Out of the Noise

OUT *of the* NOISE

A postwar childhood in a Moorlands Town

MICHAEL FISHER

The Book Guild Ltd

First published in Great Britain in 2019 by
The Book Guild Ltd
9 Priory Business Park
Wistow Road, Kibworth
Leicestershire, LE8 0RX
Freephone: 0800 999 2982
www.bookguild.co.uk
Email: info@bookguild.co.uk
Twitter: @bookguild

Typeset in 11pt Adobe Garamond Pro

Printed and bound by CPI Group (UK) Ltd, Croydon, CR0 4YY

ISBN 978 1912881 383

British Library Cataloguing in Publication Data.
A catalogue record for this book is available from the British Library.

To my two Welsh grandsons, Liam and Rhys Jones

Rhai dail ar eich coeden deulu.

CONTENTS

FOREWORD

'Leek – out of the noise' is an old expression still heard in the north-Staffordshire market town known also as 'The Queen of the Moorlands' where I spent the first twenty-five years of my life. Though some fifty or more years have now passed by, I still look upon Leek as 'home', full of memories of childhood and adolescence in that Moorlands town with its population of under 20,000. More than that, I know that many of the influences and ideas that shaped my life and future career as an historian, writer and priest, were implanted during childhood in that environment.

Another local expression, 'Leek – on a hill in a valley', is a fair description of its geography: a hill-town bounded on three sides by a broad loop of the River Churnet, and with hills encircling beyond. Each of the roads into the town dips downwards before the ascent to the top of Church Street and the Market Place. It was, and to an extent still is, a place apart, shielded by the gritstone crags and Moorlands from the industrial areas of the north, and from the Potteries by the Churnet Valley and the steep hill of Ladderedge to the south. From its highest point, crowned by the pinnacled tower of St Edward's parish church, the town falls away on all four sides, most steeply to the west where the main Buxton-

Macclesfield road cuts through the red sandstone which some consider to be the origin of the town's name, said to be derived from the Celtic *lech,* signifying rock or stone.

Until the nineteenth century, Leek retained the character of a hill-town, centred upon the church and nearby cobbled square with its livestock and produce markets as the focus of commercial activity dating back at least to the early thirteenth century when the town's rights and privileges were confirmed by King John. In the 1800s industrialisation came in the shape of textile mills leading to the town's rapid expansion on three sides, the exception being the area immediately to the north of the church, which remains open space to this day with its two public parks and sports facilities. The biggest expansion was to the east and west of the town centre, streets of terraced houses with names reflecting events and personages of the period: Waterloo Street, Wellington Street, Picton Street being amongst those at the west end. It was in this newer part of Leek that both sides of my family lived in the early years of the twentieth century. Streets in the old town bore other historic names, the main thoroughfare – Derby Street – taking its name from the Earl of Derby who acquired the manorial lordship of Leek in the sixteenth century, while neighbouring Stanley Street bore the name of the earl's family. Textile manufacturers left their imprint too: Brough Park was named after one of them, and Derby Street **[1]** is dominated by what must be one of the biggest war memorials in the country – the Nicholson clock tower, popularly known as 'The Monument', built to commemorate the fallen of World War I, and in particular Basil Nicholson, son of one of the town's leading industrialists. In the later 1800s the town's civic and commercial architecture came to be dominated by the Sugdens, a father-and-son partnership, who left their mark in the shape of many buildings in the revived 'Queen Anne' style, notably the gargantuan Nicholson Institute with its copper dome **[2]**; another gift of the silk manufacturing family. The Arts-

and-Crafts movement was an important influence within the town, and William Morris was a personal friend of another silk manufacturer, Thomas Wardle, who executed his textile designs. Their collaboration produced silk threads of superb quality, dyed with vegetable extracts producing fast colours which have stood the test of time. Meanwhile, Elizabeth Wardle and a group of ladies established the Leek Embroidery Society, using Wardle silks and metallic threads to revive long-lost needlework skills, and their work can be admired to this day in the altar-frontals, vestments and banners of the Leek churches, and indeed in others further afield, and in private collections.

Most of the textile mills have long since fallen silent, some of the buildings now serving as antiques warehouses in what has become the Antiques Capital of north Staffordshire. Though many of the town-centre shops have changed hands, some old frontages remain unaltered, and the Wednesday market still takes place on the cobbled square much as it did fifty or a hundred years ago **[3]**, with the historic 'Butter Cross' now back in the Market Place from which it had been removed in 1806 to Cornhill, south of the town and the location of the municipal cemetery. Dating from 1671, it was the gift of the Jolliffe family of Leek Hall, replacing the medieval market cross which had been damaged or destroyed during the religious upheavals of the sixteenth and seventeenth centuries. Brough Park remains as delightful as it ever was when I played there as a child and fed the swans on the lake.

With so many memories abounding, I thought to write a memoir of those bygone days for the benefit of my daughter and her family, who, naturally, know little about my early years; but I think it might be of wider interest too, and so I am happy to share these reminiscences of days just after the Second World War when people really did leave their back doors unlocked, and could walk the gas-lit streets of a Moorlands town without fear of vandals or hooligans.

Since much of what follows was not originally intended for circulation outside the family, I thought it wise to seek advice as to its suitability for publication. I am most grateful to Cathryn Walton of the Leek Historical Society and Foxlowe Arts Centre for reading the manuscript and offering sound advice; also to Neil Collingwood of Leek for his much-valued help in sourcing some of the illustrative material, and to John Murray (Publishers) Ltd. for permission to reproduce extracts from John Betjeman's *Summoned by Bells*. Thanks also to the Book Guild team for their professional editorial and marketing skills which will make it an attractive publication and so bring my story to the attention of a wider audience.

Michael Fisher

December 2018

1

MY EARLY LIFE

I was born on 25th January 1943 in the Henry Johnson ward of the North Staffordshire Royal Infirmary, the only son of Sydney (1910-1970) and Lizzie (1904-1990) Fisher; so I arrived in this world in the middle of World War II. My parents had married in September 1941 at St Edward's Church, Leek, which was their home town **[4]**. I would have had an elder brother but for the fact that my mother miscarried, and I might have had younger brothers or sisters but for the fact that my birth was difficult, and the doctors advised my parents that having any more children would be risky, and could even prove fatal. My mother was, after all, approaching 39 when I was born. So I was condemned, as it were, to being an only child. I think sometimes of the stillborn elder brother and of what he might have been to me. I have given him the posthumous name of Harry, after my mother's only brother who died in 1923 aged twenty-one.

My father was the third son of Ashley (1878-1953) and Hannah (1879-1965) Fisher. The 1901 census records my granddad's occupation as a 'cardboard box and paper cutter', and grandma's as a 'silk yarn winder'. At that time they were living with Hannah's parents in Livingstone Street, on the east side of Leek, not far from the cattle-market. They later moved to 14 Frith Street, a newly-built terrace in the west end. Like most young men at that time, my father left school (All Saints' School, Compton) at the age of fourteen, and he was apprenticed as a centre-lathe turner and fitter. It was accepted practice in working families in those days for sons still living at home to hand over their weekly pay-packets to their parents to pay for their board and lodging, receiving just a small sum back as pocket money, so there was not much left for savings. Having met and – at the age of thirty-one – married my mother, my father was the first of the brothers to move away from Frith Street to another part of the town; to no. 7 Sneyd Avenue, rented from a Mr Grindrod, verger at St Edward's Church, and previously occupied by one of the curates at the church. It was the first home I knew and where I happily spent the first eleven years of my life.

My mother's family lived at no. 3 Northcliff, an Edwardian mid-terraced house in the 'west end', which my grandparents had bought just before the First World War. The terrace backed on to Frith Street, which was lined with smaller terraced houses, and was separated from it by an open alleyway known as 'The Backs', so my mother and father were in fact near neighbours. Northcliff was a delightful house, perched, as its name implies, on the edge of a north-facing sandstone cliff. From the front of the terrace there were spectacular views over the north Staffordshire moorlands, with the towering outcrops of millstone grit known as 'The Roaches' in the distance. These houses had bay windows, entrance hall, bathroom and inside toilet, and so were a little more 'up-market' than were the ones across 'the Backs', which had none of these refinements.

My mother Lizzie (or, as she always preferred to be called, 'Betty') was the sixth of seven children born to Clifford (1864-1917) and Ellen (1864-1931) Keates. That my maternal grandparents were both thirty-one when they married (in 1895), and that my mother was their sixth child, account for that big generation gap. Looking back from the perspective of 2018, it seems extraordinary that I should have had a grandfather born as long ago as 1864, and so too old to fight in the First World War and a mother born in the same year as my wife's grandmother. Clifford Keates' life-story is told in my introduction to his published journal, *Clifford Keates: A Soldier's India* (Caron 1986). He was a joiner, soldier, poet, writer and artist of no small talent, and although he died twenty-six years before I was born, I have reason to believe that I inherited some of his characteristics, not least a diversity of interests and love of writing. His hand-written journal, entitled *From Place to Place in Foreign Lands,* is an engaging account of a 500-mile route-planning march which, as reconnaissance clerk to a Royal Artillery Field Battery, he led through the mountains, desert and jungle of north-west India in the winter of 1890. Set within this real-life adventure story, and one of its many charms, are the stories exchanged by the five soldiers as they sat around the camp fire. Sadly many of the drawings and paintings he intended as illustrations to this story either never materialised or were subsequently lost, but the surviving ones give ample testimony to his talent with pen and watercolours.

My maternal grandmother died twelve years before I was born, so what I know of her comes through my mother's and aunts' reminiscences, and from the family photograph collection. She was the eldest daughter of Micah and Hannah Carding who lived in Market Place, Leek, where my great-grandfather had a painting, decorating and plumbing business. The Cardings were well-known in Leek and the surrounding district, were deeply involved in civic affairs, and were stalwart members of the parish church. Micah Carding was an active freemason who held provincial office in the Midland Grand Lodge.

Grandma Keates was from all accounts a very gentle and endearing soul, devoted to her family, and devout in the religious sense too **[5]**. After becoming engaged to childhood sweetheart Clifford Keates in 1887, she had to say goodbye to him for seven years after he was posted to India with the Royal Artillery **[6]**, having decided somewhat rashly to join the army on the tide of patriotic fervour which had swept the country in the year of Queen Victoria's golden jubilee. His deep love for her is reflected in some of the poems he wrote at this time, such as 'Some Day', written as he prepared to leave for India in September 1888:

'I know not when I'll next meet thee,
I know not will the time be fleet,
Know not when or how 'twill be,
When two fond hearts again will meet:
I only know, deep in my soul,
Your image with life's pulse will stay,
And through dark years that onward roll,
My heart will whispering say, "Some Day".'

They continued their courtship through weekly correspondence, none of which, unfortunately, has survived, except for a verse written on a leaf plucked from a native tree, wrapped in a sheet of Royal Artillery notepaper, and sent to Ellen as a Christmas greeting:

'Oh! If thou hoveredst round my walk,
While under every well-known tree,
I to thy fancy'd shadow talk,
And every tear is full of thee.'

As well as being a thorough-going romantic, Clifford Keates had a penchant for comic verse and dry wit, and a talent for acting which led amongst other things to appearances on the stage of the Royal Artillery theatre in Ahmednagar. These elements have also appeared amongst my own character traits, and I sense his posthumous influence.

The seven-year courtship ended soon after my grandfather's return from India in the autumn of 1895. They were married at St Edward's Church, Leek, in December of that year, and set up home first in Leicester where Clifford's parents had gone to live, then moved back to Leek in 1900. Prior to enlisting he had been a carpenter and joiner, the trade to which he now returned, working for the building firm of Thomas Grace. As a craftsman he was both talented and imaginative, and in his spare time he made some splendid pieces of furniture which are still treasured in the family. Many of these were made from 'belfry oak', so called because the material came from the old bell-frames removed from the tower of St Edward's Church in 1907 when the bells were re-hung on new steel frames **[7]**. His father-in-law, Micah Carding, was churchwarden at the time, and so had the responsibility for disposing of the old frames which dated from 1721. On each item that he made, Clifford carved a bell and the dates 1721-1907. His work included a beautiful spinning chair with a pierced back and barley-sugar-twist legs, a writing-box embellished with representations of the two traceried circular windows at St Edward's **[8]**, and several stools, mirror-frames and trinket-boxes. One piece was made specially for the church: a finely-carved display-board containing the names and dates of all the vicars of Leek from the thirteenth century to the twentieth.

It would seem that I inherited some of my grandfather's artistic temperament and craft skills. In addition to drawing and painting, I developed an interest in craft work and carving, using slate rather than wood. This included the making of ornamental boxes and clock-dials – some with the same circular church window tracery as Clifford had carved in oak – and also monumental work. I was able in due course to carve a new slate memorial to my grandparents

.r family, to mark their grave in Leek Cemetery, replacing ıte marble kerb-stone that had deteriorated over the years.

ıifford Keates died in November 1917, during the First World War but not as a part of it. When the war broke out in 1914 he was almost fifty, and so too old to be drafted in. His death, preceded by distressing illness, came as a devastating blow to my grandmother. I heard it said that, after my grandfather's death my grandmother would willingly have entered a convent but for the fact that she had, singlehandedly, to look after her family of seven children. Among the family papers there is a black-edged obituary card such as it was once customary to relatives and friends of the deceased. On the envelope, in Ellen's handwriting, are the words, 'My Life's Love', which is precisely what he had been, from their childhood days in Leek, through a courtship fraught with anxiety during his seven years' absence on the other side of the world, and in twenty-two years of marriage.

A younger sister of my grandmother's lived not very far away; great-aunt Myra Carding (1874-1954) who lived alone in the house where my great-grandparents had lived in later life: Norton House, Westwood Road. 'Auntie-Auntie' as I was brought up to call her, had been engaged to a Mr Robert Ledger who had died tragically on his way back from southern Africa in about 1895. She never considered marriage again, and to the end of her life she wore the superb five-stone diamond ring that Robert Ledger had given her. The ring, and the letter commissioning it, are still in the family. I became particularly attached to the name of Carding, for its own sake and also because Auntie Myra, who was my favourite aunt, had it as her middle name. So although I received the names Michael and John at my baptism, I later pretentiously assumed – for a time at least – the name of Carding too. It was, I suppose, part of my quest for identity with those whom I considered to be the 'great and the good' of my home town; a blatant piece of juvenile snobbery which I later renounced!

My mother, as I have said, was the sixth child of a family of seven. The others were Dorothy (1896-1971), Myra (1897-1983, Nellie (1898-1975), Mary (1900-1986), Harry (1901-1923), and Florence 'Flossie' 1905-1983) **[9]**. Apart from my mother, only one of the sisters ever married, namely Mary, who in 1936 married a pharmaceutical chemist from Mansfield, Notts., John Thomas Asher (1907-1970) **[10]**. Aunties Dorothy, Myra, Nellie and Flossie continued to live in the family home at Northcliff until the end of their lives. The girls' education came to an end, as it generally did in those days, at the age of fourteen. Auntie Myra took up secretarial work, and she worked in that capacity at the textile firm of William Milner in Leek, and during the war as a clerk in the Food Office, which oversaw the issuing of ration books to every man, woman and child while rationing was in force during – and for some years after – the war. Auntie Dorothy was talented at accounting and book-keeping. Auntie Flossie served in the Women's Land Army during the war. I was told that I was rather frightened when first I saw her in uniform. Later she taught me an amusing little marching song, evidently inspired by WLA drill exercises:

'Eyes right;
form fours,
turn about;
jam for supper tonight.'

Auntie Dorothy had learned the art of fine ecclesiastical embroidery using silk and metallic threads. Leek had been rather famous for this in the later nineteenth century, and Auntie Dorothy was able to undertake the repair and restoration of a number of important altar-frontals originally executed by the Leek School of Needlework, with which two of their aunts – Myra and Susan Carding – had been involved in the late 1800s, and it was no doubt they who passed the skills on to Auntie Dorothy, along with a quantity of silks, metallic threads, and also a few finished pieces of 'Leek Embroidery' which are still amongst the family treasures. At the time of the 25th anniversary of my ordination to the priesthood, some of these pieces were applied to a vestment specially made from gold Thai silk, for use on high days and holy days.

Following the death of their mother in 1931 my aunts took over the Misses Swindells Wool and Fancy Repository Shop, 9 Stanley Street, Leek, which they kept until 1973. The shop was run by Dorothy, Nellie and Flossie, while Myra stayed at home to keep house. All four sisters had a talent for working in wool as well as selling it. They would knit jumpers, cardigans and pullovers to customers' orders, the work done mainly in the evenings back at home. One of Auntie Dorothy's specialities was rug-making. This painstaking craft involved the pulling of hundreds if not thousands of short lengths of rug-wool through a specially-prepared open-weave canvas backing – usually pre-printed with a pattern – using a special hook with a wooden handle to draw the wool through and firmly knot it in place. It was a slow process, but Auntie Dorothy had the patience, and she would happily advise beginners who wanted to give it a try. Coloured rug-wools were sold either in packs of pre-cut lengths, or in hanks which rug-makers could cut themselves using simple rotary cutting machines which were on sale at the shop. Auntie Dorothy also knitted socks, using four needles to produce seamless socks in a variety of patterns, and she would often sit knitting in the back room of the shop while the other two aunts served customers. Auntie Flossie's specialities were cardigans and jumpers. She knitted me a splendid Fair-Isle pullover in the days when such things were fashionable, and later a grey waistcoat which I still wear occasionally, some fifty years on!

Uncle John worked for John Martin, chemist, who had two shops in Leek (and one in Hanley), managing the Picton Street shop which eventually he took over in his own right. Later, after the war, he bought a former butcher's shop on the corner of West Street and Angle Street, and this became the West End Pharmacy which Uncle John operated until ill-health forced his early retirement in 1969 **[11]**. Auntie Mary and Uncle John never had children. That was not because they wanted it that way: quite the reverse, in fact. There appears to have been some medical problem. Auntie Mary was willing to undergo some tests, but I was led to believe that Uncle John was not, so there the matter rested in those days when there was no such thing as IVF, and I am not sure if they considered adoption. So, on my mother's side of the family, I was not merely an only child, but an only nephew. Having a nephew was a matter of great pride to my aunts at Northcliff, for whom the prospects of marriage and children had long since vanished, as indeed it happened to so many on account of the great numbers of men who were killed in the Great War; but Auntie Mary reacted somewhat differently, and the animosity which sometimes manifested itself between her and my mother had its roots in the fact that my mother was able to have children (or at least one) and Auntie Mary was not. I have no doubt that Uncle John would have made an excellent father, and motherhood would doubtless have softened Auntie Mary, but it was not to be. In spite of the jealousies which manifested themselves from time to time, and the fact that Auntie Mary was so different in temperament to my aunts at Northcliff, we got on reasonably well, and Uncle John had a lively sense of humour – of which more will be said later.

Uncle John and my aunts at the wool shop were members of the Leek Chamber of Trade, Uncle John being at one time chairman of this organisation which was committed to upholding good practice and the well-being of independent traders. The main commercial rival in Leek – as indeed elsewhere – was the Co-operative Wholesale Society which had several large premises in the town, and some saw it as a threat to the small retailer. Thus the Co-op was very much frowned upon by my mother's family, none of whom would ever cross its threshold, and I myself came to hold a rather prejudiced view of it until, during history lessons in school, I learned about its origins with the Rochdale Pioneers, and the great benefits that it had brought to thousands of working people. The Co-op ran its own funeral service, and I was somewhat intrigued by the advertisement in the local paper which said that those wishing to contact the undertaker out of normal shop hours should telephone the 'Green Fruit Department'.

A strange custom in Leek which I have never encountered anywhere else, was – and still is – the practice of putting printed death-notices around the town. These consist of A4 size, black-edged flyers giving the name of the deceased, and the date, time and place of the funeral, and they are displayed in various shop windows and in a glass-fronted notice-board at the east end of Derby Street. Given that the local paper, the *Leek Post and Times,* came out only weekly, and local communication was otherwise limited, I suppose it was once the most reliable way of notifying deaths and funeral arrangements, but the practice still continues. Respect for the dead is something that was drilled into me at an early age, when I was taught always to stand still and remove my cap if ever a funeral cortège passed by in the street.

The next major event after my birth was my baptism at St Edward's Church, Leek, on 21st March 1943, not that I remember it, of course! My godparents were Uncle John and Auntie Flossie. St Edward's was the main parish church of the town, 'The Old Church' as it was affectionately known **[12]**. It was where my mother's family, and especially the Cardings, had worshipped for many generations, my great-grandfather having been churchwarden there in the first decade of the twentieth century. It would have been well within Grandpa Carding's lifetime that a major restoration of the church took place, in 1867, including the complete rebuilding of the chancel to designs by the High-Victorian architect, George Edmund Street.

I was born, as I have said, during the Second World War; and although by 1943 the tide was turning in favour of the Allies, there was still a long way to go, and air-raids were a fact of life. Leek was of course something of a backwater, but enemy bombers were heard regularly overhead en route for Manchester or Liverpool, occasionally dropping the odd bomb at random. One such stray bomb killed one of my mother's cousins who lived in the west end of the town. The bomb did not actually explode, but, crashing through the roof of the house, it struck mother's cousin who was carrying his child up the stairs to bed. There was also the ever-present fear of a gas-attack, and gas-masks were kept to hand. Although eligible for active service, my father, who was a time-served centre-lathe turner and fitter, was drafted into some special war work, the exact nature of which he would never disclose. At that time he was working at the Sneyd Engineering Works, at the top of Sneyd Street and close to where we lived.

Auntie Mary and Uncle John took in a couple of evacuees as their contribution to the war effort, and Uncle John was involved with the A.R.P. (Air Raid Precaution). He also kept very detailed diaries of the war years, in which local and personal details were interwoven with his account of the progress of the war, and illustrated with press-cuttings and photographs. As a keen cinematographer, Uncle John filmed a good many local events before, during and after the war, and some of these – along with most of his diaries – are now in a local archive.

1945 saw the end of the war, and there were victory celebrations in Leek as elsewhere, but I can remember nothing of them. I was told that at the end of the VJ (Victory over Japan) celebrations in August, Uncle John ran right through the middle of the bonfire that had been lit in Lowther Place, and I could well believe it. Rationing continued for a long time afterwards, and there were shortages of all kinds of things, notably foodstuffs. We seemed always to be short of sugar, and Auntie Dorothy promised that when rationing ended she would buy us a sackful. Rationing finally ended in the early fifties, but the sack of sugar never materialised.

The first thing that I can positively remember is my aunts' wool shop in Stanley Street. I was sitting in my push-chair in the front part of the shop while my mother went into the back room to talk to one or other of my aunts. I think it was around this time that a kind lady gave me a very small teddy-bear. I became very attached to it, and it still lives with me!

No. 9 Stanley Street was a three-storey building, almost certainly designed by the Sugdens of Leek. It had deep cellars extending below the pavement. Attached to the rear of the building there was a stable in which the iron rings used long ago to tether horses could still be seen in the whitewashed walls; and above it was what had once been a hay-loft. The two storeys over the shop were spacious living quarters which my aunts rented out to tenants. I recall being invited up there occasionally, and what I remember most were the high ceilings and finely-moulded plaster cornices.

Next door to the wool shop, on the west side, was Munro's wine merchants, a double-fronted building with iron columns either side of the doorway decorated in relief with what looked like vine-scrolls with black grapes. The premises adjoining the other side of the wool shop sold wallpaper, paint and other decorating materials. While in there one day with Auntie Dorothy, I noticed a large tub containing putty, and I wondered what it was for. Auntie Dorothy bought me some to take home, to use as modelling clay (at a time when there were still postwar shortages of 'Plasticine'), perhaps not realising that putty contains linseed oil and can be quite messy. The net result was that bits of putty got trodden into the living-room carpet, was found on door-handles and chairs, and took some shifting; and with mother shouting, 'If Auntie Dorothy buys you any more putty, I'll ding it round her neck!'

On the other side of Stanley Street was 'The Bazaar', a general store operated by the Brakes family who also owned

'Freshwater Pool' – a popular outdoor lido on the road between Leek and Macclesfield. The Bazaar sold just about everything: toys, stationery, nuts and bolts, soap and other cleaning materials, pills and potions, to name but a few, some of the stock looking as though it had been there for a good many years. There was a huge central counter running all around the middle of the building, while all along the walls were glass-fronted cabinets crammed full of other merchandise.

Another of my early memories is that of being taken into St Edward's Church for some special service; it could have been Remembrance Day, but certainly the church was packed, and we sat in the big gallery at the west end. One of the hymns must have been *Eternal Father, strong to save,* for I clearly remember the words 'for those in peril on the sea' echoing around in my mind for a long time afterwards.

I cannot ever remember being afraid of the dark, but there were other childhood fears. My mother used to say that I was afraid of the moon, but that was not the whole story. It was only when the moon was on the wane that I became frightened. It seemed to me that somebody had cut a great slice off the moon. Each night it got smaller, and I thought that someone was cutting it in pieces and that it would soon all be gone. The sight of the next new moon reassured me, but then, after full moon, the same thing would happen and I could never be absolutely sure that it would come back again. Another fear was that of the dark shadow cast on the bedroom ceiling by the light-fitting, especially on light summer nights when the daylight filtered through the curtains, and the shadow seemed to move, and to get longer, as indeed it did as the sun went down. Then there was 'That Thing' in Lewis's store in Hanley. 'That Thing' was a rather clever device for sending cash and receipts backwards and forwards between the sales counters and the cashier who sat at a central desk. The money was placed in a cylinder which was then sealed and sent by compressed air through a system of tubes. When it reached its destination, the cylinder would shoot out of the tube and into a receptacle with a loud noise. This sudden noise from the snake-like contraption startled me, and I flatly refused to be taken into Lewis's for a very long time afterwards. It may have been this experience which made me afraid of any sudden loud noise, such as exploding fireworks, until I was very much older.

When I was old enough to appreciate stories, my mother would always read to me after tucking me up in bed at night, and sometimes she would make up a story of her own. Then, before she turned out the light, we would say one or two simple prayers. One of these was Charles Wesley's 'Gentle Jesus':

> Gentle Jesus, meek and mild
> Look upon a little child,
> Pity my simplicity,
> Suffer me to come to thee.

My tiny ears heard the third line as 'Pity mice in Plicity', and I sometimes went to sleep thinking of the poor mice, of what a really awful place Plicity must be, and how I must pray hard for Jesus to take pity on them, and let them out.

It seems that, as a small child, I had quite a remarkable memory. Dad had a collection of cigarette cards, some of which were pictures of famous footballers and cricketers. I was told that he would sit me on his knee, hold up a card, and I would repeat the relevant name after him. After a little practice he could hold up any picture and I would be able to put the right name to it, much to the amazement of friends and neighbours who nicknamed me 'Mr Memory'.

Toys were, like everything else just after the war, in short supply, but my father was able to compensate by making things for me out of wood or metal. The spare bedroom at Sneyd Avenue was kitted-out as a workshop, complete with a workbench which

Dad made himself, a lathe and fretsaw; not perhaps a very practical arrangement, and my mother was forever complaining about wood-shavings and sawdust being trodden into the landing and stair carpets. Out of that workshop came such things as a rocking swan which appears in some early snapshots with me sitting on it **[13]**; later a scooter, a splendid iron-framed toboggan, a bedside lamp in the shape of an old-fashioned gas-lamp, a toy crane, and – the pride of them all – a steam-engine made out of gleaming brass and copper. Sadly, this is the only item from those early years that I still have **[14]**; but growing up with tools around me meant that I learned all kinds of things from observation, and some of those same tools are still in use, as is my father's workbench which I acquired after his death in 1970.

In addition to toy-making, my father made some items of furniture for the house. There was a tea trolley, the frame of which was made from gleaming copper tubing, with trays of polished oak. Pride of place was given to a long-case clock with an electrically-powered pendulum movement. Dad made the case from light oak, and the dial was furnished with numerals cut from sheet brass. The movement of the pendulum was governed by an electro-magnet which was triggered to cut in every minute or so to boost its momentum. It kept perfect time. He also invented a handbag hook. Ladies were sometimes at a loss as to where to put their handbags when out for a meal in a restaurant, or at a whist-table. Dad came up with the idea of a G-shaped device made from 3mm diameter plastic-covered metal rod, substantial, but small enough to fit into a lady's handbag. The upper end of the 'G' was fixed into a padded metal disc which sat on the table-top, with the lower end curving down under the table to form a hook from which the handbag could be suspended safely but within easy reach of its owner. He made several of these for my mother and her sisters, and I'm sure that he could have made a commercial success of it, had he chosen to do so.

I have no doubt that, given the right opportunities, Dad's varied skills could have earned him more money than ever he was paid by his employers. He worked with great precision at whatever he did, expected the same high standards of those he worked with and helped to train, and he didn't suffer fools gladly. While working for the engineering firm of F. Bode on Buxton Road, he was involved with the design and construction of a machine which was able to cut blocks of ice-cream to precise dimensions within a thousandth of an inch. It had great potential for large-scale production purposes and with obvious economic benefits to the manufacturer. I can remember seeing a photograph of this machine, with my father and other members of the firm standing by, but I have no idea what subsequently became of it.

There was never any question of my mother going out to work, as some mothers did even in those far-off days when it was still widely believed that 'a woman's place is in the home'. Like her sisters, my mother could knit, sew and embroider, and she did for a time take on some out-work for the textile firm of Job White, on Compton. I would generally go with her to fetch parcels of yarn and to return the finished garments. Some of these consisted of string vests, which she knitted on large wooden needles. At one time Whites were producing costumes for a film company which was making some kind of medieval epic, and I clearly remember mother knitting lots of 'chain-mail' for battle scenes using silver metallic-coated string, and very convincing they looked, but the silvering tended to rub off on her fingers as she worked, and it took some removing.

No. 7 Sneyd Avenue was a small three-bedroomed semi-detached house built in the 1930s which my parents rented from a private landlord. It was on a corner where the avenue turned right, so there was what in those days seemed a huge garden between us and the Hammersleys who lived at no. 9. Just beyond the corner the avenue rose fairly steeply upwards before coming to a dead end in a turning-circle at the top: ideal, as I later discovered, for riding scooters and go-carts downhill, and for sledging in winter. There were precious few cars around in the 1940s, so it was quite safe to play in the avenue. Milk was still delivered in the old-fashioned way. Mr Hulme – a dairy farmer on Buxton Road – would come round with a horse-drawn wagon and dispense the milk out of a churn into the jugs which our mothers brought out. There was a corner shop at the bottom of Sneyd Street from which we bought bread in large unwrapped and – of course unsliced – loaves. When sent down to fetch a loaf I would sometimes nibble off the corners on the way back. The town was only a few minutes' walk away – out of the avenue, up Sneyd Street, then into the oddly-named Strangman Street and so into the main thoroughfares, but to a small child, going 'up town' was something of an expedition, undertaken on the weekly market-day when most of the other shopping was done.

The house at Sneyd Avenue had a fair-sized garden at the side of the house, and room for a small greenhouse. My father was quite a keen gardener. He grew tomatoes in the greenhouse, and a variety of vegetables in the garden, including runner beans. Very few people had refrigerators in those days, so vegetables and fruit were preserved in airtight 'Kilner' jars. The beans were sliced and then packed into the jars between layers of salt. The jars were stowed away in what mother called the 'squirrel cupboard' in the spare bedroom, along with bottled fruit, and jars of the blackberry jelly which she made after our fruit-picking outings to Hillswood in the autumn.

There were altogether about twenty-four houses in Sneyd Avenue. I can still remember the names of most of the people who lived there, and some of them had children of around my own age, so I was not short of playmates. There was the Rowlands family at no. 1; they had two girls, Sylvia and Angela. Then there were the Cotterills at no. 3: no children but, unusually, a car which came out only at weekends. The number-plate contained the letters BNA, so it was nicknamed 'the banana car'. Next door at no. 5 were Bill and Vera Buxton and their children Pat and Alan. There were the Hollinsheads at no. 15, and their son Barry (not to be confused with unrelated James Hollinshead who comes into my story later). Next door at no. 17 were the Masseys who had two children, Arthur and Elizabeth. There were much older children too, such as Laura Seed, Margaret Ward, and Audrey Trafford who was the daughter of butcher Wilf Trafford who lived at no. 12 and was the only other person in the avenue to own a car at that time. No. 14 was occupied by two schoolmistresses: Miss Abbott, whom I was to encounter at primary school, and Miss Booth who taught at the local girls' secondary modern.

When it came to schools, there was a very good choice available in Leek. There were the various denominational schools such as the Parish Church School which my mother and aunts had gone to; Catholic and Methodist schools, and there was Westwood Road County Primary School which was where I was sent. Built just before the war it was set on the western edge of the town, with large open spaces and playing fields all around. It had the disadvantage of being quite some distance away from where we lived, so until I was old enough to come and go on my own, my mother had to trek there and back four times a day. School dinners in those days – apart from being quite revolting – were considered only for those who could not possibly get home at midday, or whose mothers were out at work. I remember how mothers would gather outside the gates of the infants' entrance in the afternoon, and how some of them would remove dirt from their offsprings' grubby faces by spitting on a handkerchief and rubbing vigorously.

My first teacher in the infants' class was Constance Winifred Arkcoll; a good teacher, no doubt, but sharp as mustard and, as they say, a bit of a tartar too. I was always somewhat afraid of Miss Arkcoll, and sometimes felt victimised but I learned. The primary objective in those days was to get children to read and write and do simple arithmetic as quickly as possible, and she certainly succeeded in that. There were games and stories too. I remember Miss Arkcoll reading us the story of The Gingerbread Man, and we all got our mothers to make gingerbread men which we then took to school. I later learned of a sad side to Connie Arkcoll's life. She had been engaged for years to a Mr Vincent Rabone whose father – a Lay Reader at St Edward's Church – objected strongly to the relationship because Connie was Roman Catholic, so the marriage did not take place until after old Harvey Rabone had died. Thus I learned my first lesson in the awful field of religious bigotry. It irritated me even as a child, and it still makes me sad and angry if I encounter it now. Whenever I pass the Rabone family grave on visits to Leek cemetery, I cannot resist a wry smile, knowing that Connie's remains now lie buried on top of those of the bigoted Harvey!

From Miss Arkcoll's class we moved up to Miss Abbot, the near-neighbour to whom I have already referred; and then to Miss Rogers, a dear lady who was immensely popular and always seemed to have a crowd of children around her. She lived in Waterloo Street, which was the way many of us walked to and from school and more often than not a group of us would walk along with her. She was very much an 'auntie' figure, full of interesting stories and anecdotes. One of the things I remember most clearly is that at Christmas time she would bring in an old umbrella which she had painted silver. The umbrella would be suspended from the classroom ceiling, and on the end of each spoke Miss Rogers would hang a coloured glass bauble: an unusual and magical object it seemed to seven- and eight-year-olds.

Christmas-time at Westwood Road was altogether magical. There was the learning of Christmas songs and carols, making paper-chains and paper lanterns to decorate the classroom, and then – the climax of it all – the school Christmas party. There were games, there was food, there was singing, and it all seemed to go on late into the evening although in reality it was probably all over by about seven o'clock. One of the highlights was a kind of variation on the 'Konga'. All of us would join hands, the piano would strike up, and we would dance off in a huge snake formation down the corridors, weaving in and out of the classrooms, and eventually back to the hall; all the time singing a song about a little Dutch girl and a little Dutch boy:

> 'And the little old mill went round and round
> And round went the little old mill'

– was the chorus at the end of each verse. There was the occasional fancy-dress party too, and I remember appearing rather unconvincingly as Old Mother Riley, one of my cinema favourites played by the comedian Arthur Lucan.

One of the other highlights of the year was Sports Day on the big field. There were all the usual children's events such as the sack race, egg-and-spoon race, three-legged race, and so on. There was also a percussion band, presided over by Miss Arkcoll who would sit at the piano and play tunes in various rhythms which we would accompany on tambourines, triangles and drums, forty of us at a time. The sound must have been excruciating, and I can understand why Connie Arkcoll was sometimes in a bad mood. But it was an introduction to music, and we all learned through this exercise how to read a simple musical score. There were also singing lessons, taken by a Miss Heath, with Connie A at the piano of course, and we went through a medley of English folk songs such as 'Bobby Shaftoe', 'Lavender's Blue', and patriotic ones such as 'Land of Hope and Glory'.

The school day began with an assembly presided over by the headmaster, Mr Stephenson. It included formal prayers and a scripture reading, and it was not unknown for Mr Stephenson to call out a pupil who he suspected of being inattentive, and ask him or her to give a resumé of what had been read. Morning and afternoon school normally ended with prayers in class, preceded by the teacher's instruction, 'Hands together and eyes closed'.

Other teachers through whose hands I passed included Miss Tomlinson who was a friend of Auntie Dorothy's, and also a member of St Edward's Church, and Mrs Pickering who taught our class for the last two years at Westwood Road. Class-teaching in junior schools in those days involved the whole curriculum, so the class teachers taught us English, arithmetic, and almost everything else. There was no such thing as science, geography and history in any well-defined sense; these subjects simply 'occurred' in the general curriculum; and there was not even an attempt to introduce a foreign language. English, however, was taught with great care, with much emphasis on correct spelling and punctuation; and I think it is fair to say that no-one left Westwood Road Primary School without knowing how to construct a proper sentence, and without a reasonable vocabulary. Would that all eleven-year-olds reached the same standard nowadays.

Class sizes in schools have become something of an issue in recent times, and thirty is considered excessive. A photograph taken in about 1952 **[15]** shows the class I was in at Westwood Road numbered forty, most of whose names I can still remember, but I cannot say that we felt disadvantaged. There was a happy atmosphere about the school; there was order and gentle discipline, good manners were expected and instilled. I do not recall there being any really troublesome pupils, and child psychiatrists and social workers were virtually unknown, but then in those days pressures upon young children were far fewer than is the case today, and when family units were much more stable such pressures could be absorbed and dealt with. Single-parent families were almost unknown, except in rare cases of the early demise of one of the parents, and divorce was generally frowned upon. The notion of the 'extended family' in which grandparents, uncles and aunts all had a role in children's upbringing is now of the past; yet my own experience tells me how very valuable these relationships were throughout childhood and indeed beyond it.

It was while at Westwood Road that I made my first attempts at creative writing. One of these was a brief history of St Edward Confessor, to whom the parish church was dedicated, and of the church itself, gleaned from what I had learned from the vicar, the Revd. Norman Watson, who was a keen historian, and from guidebooks. My first literary success came at the tender age of eight, when I won a prize in a story-writing competition organised by the RSPCA. The story had to involve animals or birds, and so I spun a tale about the adventures of an escaped budgerigar. A representative of the RSPCA came to the school to present the prize – one of Enid Blyton's *Secret Seven* adventure books, and this has remained on my bookshelf as a treasured possession, and a reminder of how my literary career began all those years ago.

The influences most at work on me at school as well as within the family appear to have been predominantly female, but not exclusively so. The headmaster of Westwood Road School was Mr Stephenson, followed by Mr Hartley. Both were involved in class-teaching as well as administration, and they would sometimes take over from the regular teacher for a morning or an afternoon. Then there were Mr Hyde and Mr Whittingham. Mr Hyde's speciality, as I remember, was English, and he could tell some rattling good stories. Mr Whittingham took the boys of the class for football, which I quite enjoyed; and he also taught drawing, painting and handicraft. I remember he taught us elementary bookbinding; how to make a hardbacked notebook with stitched-in pages.

Apart from the outdoor games and sports, physical education consisted of what was then called 'Drill'; quite literally knees-bend arms-stretch types of exercise. P.E. kit consisted of a pair of black plimsolls and a bean-bag, and the only gymnastic apparatus I can recall is a set of parallel bars. We also did 'Rhythmics', physical exercises set to music, and I remember that there was a weekly radio programme called Music and Movement which the teacher tuned in to, and we followed the exercises. For games and other activities, the school was divided into 'houses' denoted by colours. There were the Blues, the Greens, the Reds and the Yellows. During games and other physical activities, everyone wore a braid of the appropriate colour, placed over the left shoulder and under the right arm. Each class was divided into teams of ten or so, each with its leader, and team leaders wore two crossed braids. Competition was encouraged between the colours, and in the hall there was a Merit Board divided into four calibrated columns, one for each colour, and a set of sliding indicators showed who was ahead. At the side of the merit board was a framed picture of a dog named Patch. His collar had a detachable bow, and there were four of these, one in each of the colours. So if the Reds reached the top of the board first, Patch would have a red bow attached, and there it would stay as the indicators on the board were all set back to zero and the process started all over again.

Whether because of my Uncle John's profession, or because of reading, I became very interested in science. I had a chemistry set at home, and would mix all kinds of foul concoctions, often without really knowing what I was doing; also some explosive mixtures from which I made fireworks, the ingredients being packed into cardboard sweet-tubes. It was incredibly easy in those days to obtain the necessary ingredients – such as potassium nitrate and sodium chlorate – over the counter. Early one Sunday morning an experiment with a lighted candle went horribly wrong, and the curtains in the living room went up in flames. The result was somewhat painful: the only good hiding I ever received from my father, and being sent off to Sunday School every week. I don't know which hurt the most!

An equally spectacular accident for which I was not directly responsible was the night the Christmas tree caught fire. I imagine I was about ten years old at the time, and one December afternoon my mother suggested it was time to get out the Christmas decorations and put up the tree. The tree was a small artificial one which Auntie Flossie had given us for my first Christmas, and it was thus held in some veneration. So it was fetched from the spare room where it lived between Christmasses, removed from the wrappings in which it was always reverently packaged, and placed on a small table in the bay window of the front room. At the ends of the branches there were candle-holders in which small wax candles were placed, but of course they were never lit. I asked my mother if we might light them just for a few minutes. I cannot remember whether this was before or after the living-room curtains fire, but anyhow mother agreed, 'Just this once, and just for a few minutes'. One by one the candles were lit, until the tree with its tinsel and baubles shimmered in the darkened room – a piece of real Christmas magic, so I thought.

I was then sent off to Cooper's newsagents on the corner of Sneyd Street and Broad Street to fetch the *Evening Sentinel*. It was only a few minutes' errand, and I ran all the way there and all the way back, hoping that the tree would still be alight in the window when I returned. It was, but not in the way I had expected. As I ran towards the gate I saw the reflection of flames in the front window. A neighbour was standing with one foot over the doorstep, calling out, 'Can you manage, Betty?' Then mother appeared, carrying at arm's length the blazing Christmas tree. Narrowly missing the neighbour, she hurled the towering inferno out of the door and on to a flower-bed where it was left to burn itself out.

How my mother escaped serious injury I will never know. It appeared that while I was out at the newsagent's, she had gone into the kitchen to put the kettle on, leaving the tree and its lighted candles unattended. A draught from the door had done the rest.

Soon afterwards my father came home from work. We had to tell him about the fire, of course, although the smouldering remains in the flower-bed told their own story. He was not without a sense of humour, and eventually he saw the funny side of what could so easily have been a tragedy. He decided to play a practical joke on Auntie Flossie who was due to call on us that evening. He went outside and retrieved the charred remains of the tree. What a pathetic thing it now looked: only the trunk was left, with blackened wires where the branches had been, and a few shattered decorations.

'Let's wrap it up again,' Dad said, 'then when auntie comes tonight we can tell her that we've decided not to bother with the tree this year, and ask her if she wants it back.' So when Auntie Flossie arrived the brown-paper parcel was put in front of her, but in the end our nerve failed and we felt obliged to unwrap it, revealing the cremated remains. The expression on her face may better be imagined than described.

When I came downstairs the next morning I found an envelope containing some money and a note from Dad telling me to go to Talbot's shop in Fountain Street, where real Christmas trees were on sale, and to get one. So Christmas that year was not as bad as I thought it was going to be. Mr Cooper, the newsagent, soon heard about the incident, and he never let me forget the night the tree went up in flames. For years afterwards he would pull my leg by asking, 'Ast thay 'ad any mower fires?' and, 'ow's thi' flamin' Christmas tray?'

Mr Cooper's broad north-Staffordshire accent reminds me that the area had – and still has – an ancient dialect that is quite distinct from that of the Potteries ten miles or so to the south. It has its peculiar quirks and expressions, many of which were catalogued over a hundred years ago by local historian M.H. Miller, in his classic *Olde Leeke* (1891), who traced some of them back to Shakespearean times. Among the dialect's characteristics are crystal-clear enunciation of vowels and consonants: there's no swallowing of word-endings, and – until recently – no sign of that infectious aberration, the 'glottal stop'. Sadly, however, and largely through TV soaps such as *Eastenders* and *The Only Way is Essex,* regional dialects are suffering as so-called Estuary English spreads ever northwards, with its inability to pronounce the letter 't'. There is all the difference in the world between regional dialects and plain slovenliness. Dialects are a vital part of our cultural heritage. Essex is *not* the only way, and I think there is a strong case for the formation of an organisation called *SPADE* (Society for the Preservation of the Ancient Dialects of England) before it's too late.

In addition to the dialect, there were some odd expressions in use that I've never heard anywhere else, such as 'rowking round', meaning wandering around the house aimlessly at night; an incessant talker was called a 'clock-cleaner'; a promiscuous male was known as a 'rumptifizzer'; a 'hoppit' was an untidy house, and the dustbin was commonly known as the 'ash-box'. Some proper names were habitually mispronounced, e.g. A-*rundle* rather than Arun-del, and B'*mont* for Beaumont, while Macclesfield was almost always *Mackless*-field.

2

THE FORMATIVE YEARS

Back in the 1950s there was little by way of ready-made entertainment. We had a radio, but television sets were few and far between. The first of the family to have one were Auntie Mary and Uncle John who bought one in time for the Coronation in 1953. There were wind-up gramophones, but no 'pop' music directed towards youngsters, or teenage fashions. Not until Bill Hayley and the Comets burst on the scene in the 1950s with *Rock Around the Clock* was there any serious attempt by the music industry to exploit children and teenagers commercially. For one thing, there wasn't much money around. There was a wind-up gramophone at Northcliff, and my aunts had quite a collection of records dating mainly from the 1930s. There were records of comic songs which amused me, for example, 'Why is the Bacon so Tough?', 'Ain't it Grand to be Bloomin' well Dead?' and 'I've Never Squeezed a Lemon like You', some of which I have kept. There was some serious music too, vocal, choral and instrumental, and I came to have an appreciation of music at quite an early age.

We also used to listen to music, amongst other things, on the radio. In those days at Sneyd Avenue my mother and I would sit in the front room on Sunday evenings (Sunday being the only day when a fire was lit in the front room in winter) and tune in to the Palm Court Orchestra which played selections from popular classics. My father meanwhile went out to the pub. Other favourite radio programmes included *Educating Archie,* Archie being a ventriloquist's dummy; but whoever heard of a radio ventriloquist?! These were the last years of ITMA (short for 'It's That Man Again') starring the comedian Tommy Handley. For excitement there was *Dick Barton,Special Agent*, while *Journey into Space*, a weekly series starring Andrew Faulds as 'Jet Morgan' was an absolute must for all boys of my age; and there was of course *Children's Hour*, a magazine-type programme which was the radio precursor of later TV series such as *Blue Peter*. That long-running radio soap-opera *The Archers,* began in the early 1950s, following the demise of Dick Barton.

Holidays in the '40s and early '50s were few; there wasn't the money to spare. When I was four years old we spent a week in a caravan owned by a friend of Uncle John at Abergele. A photograph taken at this time shows me playing with pebbles from the beach, and my mother sitting in a deck-chair and calling out some instructions **[16]**. Looking at this photograph some years later, and noting the expression on mother's face, my father made the comment, 'She looks just like the Belsen kommandant'! Kind and loving as my mother was, and fun-loving too, she was also strong-minded, and given to issuing orders both to myself and to Dad; 'She who must be obeyed'!

I remember one or two holidays at Lytham St Annes, where there was a huge beach, but you had to walk out a long way to get to the sea. Dad became quite an expert at sand sculpture. As well as the usual sandcastles he would build lighthouses and model boats big enough for me to sit in **[17]**. Nearby was Fairhaven Lake, where there were sailing-boats and motor-boats for hire.

There were day-trips of course, some with Uncle John and Auntie Mary who were the only ones in the family with a car, and some by bus. Llandudno was a favourite destination, although it took a long time to get there in those days; also Blackpool and Southport. Buxton was nearer at hand, although the twelve-mile journey by bus seemed to take a long time too, up over the moors past the Roaches, and in summer the engine of the bus would sometimes overheat when going up the long steep hill at Upperhulme, and the driver would have to stop amid clouds of steam to let it cool off or to put more water in the radiator. We would sometimes also take the bus to Warslow, from where it was only a short walk down into the Manifold Valley. Mrs Massey and Arthur would usually come with us. Dorothy Massey was one of my mother's best friends as well as being a near neighbour, and Arthur was my best friend during those years at Sneyd Avenue.

Dorothy Massey was a lively, entertaining, and well-read lady who seemed to spot my potential for science, and just before I moved up to Leek High School she kindly gave me three new books, on chemistry, physics, and biology, thinking that they might be useful as indeed they proved to be, and I kept hold of them long after I had left school. Another near neighbour, a teacher named Mr Robinson, gave me a complete set of Charles Dickens as he and his family prepared to move house, and so, even while still at junior school, I was introduced to Dickens' caricatured portrayal of life in Victorian England, with its larger-than-life characters. I can also remember listening on the radio to a serialised reading of Anthony Trollope's, *The Last Chronicle of Barset:* a rich diet for a ten-year-old.

Arthur Massey was a cub-scout in the 2nd Leek pack which met in the scout headquarters off Stockwell Street. I thought I might give it a try, and so was kitted out with the necessary uniform. I have to say that I never really took to it, and discontinued after about twelve months. Church parades normally ended up in one or other of the town's Methodist chapels which I thought were somewhat dull and dowdy compared with the splendours of the parish church. Methodism was strongly represented in the town with large chapels: Ball Haye Green, Brunswick chapel in Market Street, Bethesda in Ball Haye Street, Mill Street Ragged School chapel, and the local 'cathedral' of Methodism, Mount Pleasant on Clerk Bank, and there was also West Street Infant and Junior School. Arthur Massey's family were active members of 'The Mount', and his father was a local preacher.

Ten miles from Leek in the opposite direction from Buxton was Hanley, the nearest large town and the one to which Leek people would naturally gravitate for specialist shopping, for the department stores like Lewis's, Huntbaches and Bratt & Dykes. A day out in Hanley on the bus was always something of a treat, and it seemed to take an eternity to travel the twelve miles between the towns. In the days before the Clean Air Act everything was coal-fired including the many bottle-ovens of the pottery works, and it was quite a sight to see these in full smoke. Likewise the red glow from the Shelton Steel Works, and there were the gigantic coal-tips on the northern approach to the Potteries via Baddeley Green and Cobridge. Hanley was where Santa Claus lived in the run-up to Christmas, in his grotto at Lewis's, and the Christmas season always finished with a visit to the pantomime at the Theatre Royal. It was nevertheless considered by Leek people to be almost a foreign country where people spoke differently – 'Up 'Anley, duck' – and marrying a so-called 'Pot-herb' was thought by many to be a step down the social ladder.

Living in Leek meant that open country was within walking distance. Not very far away was the canal basin which was the terminus of the Leek branch of the Cauldon Canal. Walks along the canal towards Cheddleton, or along the feeder stream which supplied water from Rudyard Lake, either in the company of my parents or with school-friends, were a regular pastime. On the north side of the town was Hillswood, a vast open area of grassland, heathland and woodland which for me and my friends was one huge adventure playground where we could fancy ourselves as explorers, adventurers, cowboys and Indians, or whatever took our fancy. Towards the top of Hillswood, and away from the main pathway, was a kind of shallow ravine – left, I think, from quarrying operations in the dim and distant past; now it served us as a mini 'Grand Canyon'. There was an abundance of large stones, from which we would construct rudimentary huts, roofing them in with branches cut from nearby trees, and ferns. Summer picnics were plenty, and Hillswood served us well with blackberries and mushrooms in the autumn, and firewood in the winter. Between the lower slopes of Hillswood and the River Churnet lies Abbey Farm and the ruins of the medieval Dieulacres Abbey **[18]** which even in those early years fired my imagination, especially the legends of buried treasure and of a secret tunnel leading to St Edward's Church in Leek.

A companion on many of these expeditions was the little dog, Nell, which my parents acquired for me in the summer of 1953. Black and white, part spaniel and part something else, she was a lively little soul, and loved those long walks on Hillswood where there were lots of rabbit-holes and other things for her to investigate.

Sometimes the countryside came to us, such as on the Wednesday market-days when stallholders would pack the Leek Market Place, and people would come in to town from the surrounding villages. Wednesday was always the busiest day at the wool shop when the country people would come in to buy their wools and patterns, sometimes bringing in boxes of eggs, packets of farm-produced butter, and poultry. I dare say a little bartering went on! In addition to the stalls in the square, there was (and still is) a covered market-hall with a variety of stalls, and beyond it is the Butter Market, a large open hall where – as the name implies – farmers would come to sell their produce, including – as I remember – live hens and newly-hatched chicks. The Butter Market was also used as an alternative wet-weather venue for community events scheduled for the Market Place. Advertising posters would often state, 'If wet, in the Butter Market'. This expression passed into common parlance, for example when arranging to meet friends in the town at a certain time and place, someone might add, '…and if wet, in the Butter Market'!

During school holidays I would almost invariably go 'up town' with my mother on Wednesday mornings, and we would go round the market. There would sometimes be a stop at Tatton's Café in Derby Street for a glass of lemonade and a sausage roll, and then on to the Cattle Market which at that time was at the bottom end of the town, in Hayward Street where the bus station and Smithfield shopping centre now stand**[19]**. Wednesday was not Wednesday without a trip around the pens to see the cattle, sheep and pigs. The Cattle Market was also the venue for the May Fair which visited the town annually, with roundabouts, swingboats, cake-walks and the usual sideshows. I remember that a lot of the smaller children's rides in those days were hand-cranked, so the operators worked hard for their money.

Sadly, Tatton's Café is no more. It fell victim to the wave of legalised vandalism which swept across the country as a whole from the 1960s onwards, as many a town centre was 're-developed'. The not unreasonable desire to inject new life into a town, including the provision of more car-parking space, was accompanied by a lack of sensitivity towards heritage buildings and matters of design. Tatton's was an early victim. True, it was 'mock-Tudor' and of no outstanding architectural merit, but it was a valued part of the built environment, harmonising with both the genuinely seventeenth-century timber-framed Roebuck Inn adjacent to it on one side, and the Sugden-designed District Bank on the other. The modernist horror which replaced it sticks out like the proverbial sore thumb, or, as HRH The Prince of Wales might say, 'a carbuncle' on the face of the fair town. Other casualties of the time included the Victorian town hall and the neo-Gothic Brunswick chapel, both in nearby Market Street **[2]**. Not for nothing did the Moorlands District Council twice receive the *Private Eye* Philistine Council of the Year accolade for its attempted 'Rape of a Moorlands Queen'.

Another great attraction in my junior school days was Leek Railway Station, quite a busy place with a large shunting-yard. Leek was on the picturesque Churnet Valley line **[20]**, and there were also connections to main lines via Stoke and Macclesfield, until it all fell under Dr Beeching's 'axe' in the 1960s. This was still the age of steam of course, and there was something awesome about one of these iron monsters issuing from the mouth of the Westwood tunnel in a cloud of smoke and steam. In junior school days Auntie Nellie would meet me along Westwood Road on Thursday afternoons – Thursday was half-day closing in Leek, and the wool shop was closed – and we would sometimes go down to the station and watch the trains. Occasionally I got to ride on the footplate of one of the shunting engines, and we would sometimes take a train out of Leek, get off a few stations down, such as Stockton Brook, and then come back to Leek on the bus. Needless to say, all I ever wanted to become in those days was an engine-driver.

Although I was once photographed in the driving-seat of a narrow-gauge steam-engine on some family outing, the only train I ever got to operate was a model one. It was an 'O' gauge Hornby layout, with two-inch track, and when all set up it took up the entire front room at Sneyd Avenue. There was a splendid tinplate station with little doors that opened, and chimneys. My mother, who was a cigarette-smoker in those days, would sometimes puff smoke through one of the doors, so that it would come out through the chimney. There was also a signal box, signals and a tunnel, and a variety of rolling-stock. The trouble was that the engine would only operate on A.C. mains electricity, and Leek in those days was on the old D.C. (Direct Current) generated at the town electricity works. A conversion scheme was in prospect, but it was slow in coming. So in the meantime I had to operate my railway by pushing the trucks and carriages around the track by hand, and the engine remained firmly in its wooden box. Then, around Christmas – the Christmas after the great Tree Fire – Dad came home with a large and mysterious object which he said was a converter. It would convert the D.C. electricity into A.C. and so we would be able to run the train. The converter was duly set up in the coal-house, cables were connected, the railway layout was assembled for the first time with the engine on the track, and wired up to the transformer. To begin with all seemed to go well, and both Dad and I were thrilled to see the train running around the track, or reversing into a siding with a complement of trucks. Then, suddenly, we heard a dull 'bang' coming from the direction of the coal-house. All the lights went out, the train stopped, and it was clear that something had gone seriously wrong. A glance through the window told us that the lights in neighbouring houses had gone out too. The next morning the 'converter', or whatever it was, was discreetly removed and a veil was drawn over the proceedings. Not long afterwards the town was put on A.C. electricity, so the train ran again – legally.

Winters in Leek always seemed colder, with far more frost and snow about than one sees nowadays. There was the notorious winter of 1947 when there was snow around from January to March, but I have only the vaguest memory of it. Every winter, however, brought snowfalls, generally after Christmas, and outlying villages, especially on the Buxton side of Leek, would get cut off. We children had a whale of a time. Sneyd Avenue was, as

I have already mentioned, ideal for sledging, and the long slopes of Leek Park were always thronged with children and sledges. The Westwood Recreation Ground, which lay on the school route, was also popular for winter sports of a different kind. Groups of children would build big barricades of compacted snow, and rival 'gangs' would emerge from behind them to try to take the 'enemy' barricade by storm, while the defenders would repel the attackers with volleys of snowballs.

In the days when central heating in private homes was the exception rather than the rule, coal fires were the norm. At 7 Sneyd Avenue, even in the winter, only one fire was normally lit, the one in the living room which also provided hot water through the back boiler. Sundays were the exception, when we had tea in the front room and a fire was lit, when appropriate, in a small corner-grate. We had at least one electric fire, but that was about it. The upstairs rooms were unheated even in winter, and I remember the atmosphere and wet walls of the steam-filled bathroom on winter bath-nights; also waking up in the morning to find that 'Jack Frost' had created his wondrous fern-like patterns in the frozen condensation on the insides of the windows.

Family visiting was a regular part of my childhood. Everyone lived nearby, within walking distance, the most distant relatives being Auntie Mary and Uncle John who lived in Lowther Place, off the Ashbourne Road, in the house they had had built at the time of their marriage in 1936. Dad would always visit his parents in Frith Street on Sunday mornings, and I usually went along with him, or, in the days after I joined St Edward's choir, I would meet him there after church. We would then go across the 'backs' to Northcliff and spend an hour there before going home for lunch. Dad thought very highly of my aunts, and was always ready and willing to do any odd jobs around the house.

Although church-going had declined, Sunday was generally observed in those days as a day of rest reserved for family activities.

Apart from the odd newsagent, shops remained firmly closed, and the cinemas were closed too. The town itself, and the residential areas, were quiet and largely deserted. I remember how dogs' barking echoed around the streets on a Sunday as at no other time. Licensed premises had Sunday opening times, and after visiting my grandparents and aunties, Dad and I would sometimes call in the West Street Working Men's Club (of which mother did not really approve) where he would have a pint of beer, and I would have a 'Vimto', or something similar. Located at the top end of West Street, near to its junction with Mill Street, the club was a strange building in that one entered at street level, but then descended a flight of stairs to the main bar on the level below. This was because the ground on which it was built shelved down steeply on the Mill Street side. As I remember, the bar was equipped with glazed shutters, rather like sash-windows, which were brought down at closing-time, and there were round-topped tables with ornate cast-iron legs, under some of which were white enamelled bowls of sawdust: i.e. *spittoons.* No wonder my mother disapproved, not that she ever deigned to set foot in there!

The location of my aunts' house at Northcliff, on the edge of a rocky decline, high above the main Belle Vue road, meant that the front entrance was via a gateway part-way down the hill, with flights of steps leading up to the terrace. In practical terms this meant that the front door was rarely opened, and family, friends, neighbours and tradesmen invariably used the rear entrance via the 'backs'. Though on friendly terms with the other families in the terrace, my aunts never went in for what they called 'neighbouring', i.e. being forever in and out of one another's houses. That does not mean they were inhospitable, for they frequently invited close friends to tea, at which a selection of Auntie Myra's freshly-baked cakes were generally on offer.

On the Northcliff side of 'the backs', the terrace consisted of eight or nine houses. Neighbouring families included old Mrs Tatton, a white-haired lady who lived at no. 4; the Thompsons on the end of the terrace at no. 1, and Walter and Jessie Bailey three doors up from my aunts. Both the Thompsons and the Baileys were staunch Methodists, the Baileys in particular being 'big at the chapel' as the saying went, and their daughter married a Wesleyan minister. One of my aunts told the story of an incident which caused considerable embarrassment when my cousin Beryl, being asked by the Baileys what she wanted to be when she grew up, replied, 'I want to be a *Ranter Methody*'.

I too, it seemed, had the ability to shock by coming out with odd expressions and jokes, a little risqué perhaps, though never, I believe, rude or vulgar ones. The object was to elicit what I termed an *out-gasp*. 'Michael!' – one of the company would exclaim in a disapproving half-spoken, half-whispered exhalation of breath of which 'out-gasp' is not a bad description – *'Michael!!'* The out-gasp would more often than not be accompanied by raised eyebrows and a feigned-pained facial expression which barely concealed an inner desire to laugh or snigger. Indeed, when I made an excuse to leave the room, I could hear chuckles and outright laughter coming from the other side of the door, so I knew I had scored a hit. I am reminded of a remark once made by a fellow-soldier about my grandfather Clifford: 'I've heard him say things to officers that other men would get six months for, but they only laugh at him.' Though as a youngster I was known to be somewhat diffident and reticent in other circumstances, I never once suffered from stage-fright, and would gladly stand up, dress up, and perform. I have seen this come out too in my youngest grandson, who is a born mimic, and who rarely misses an opportunity to raise a laugh.

Mother and I generally went to Northcliff for tea on Mondays after school. Monday was always 'washing day'. Things being generally quiet at the wool shop on Monday mornings, Auntie Dorothy would stay at home and help with the washing. There was a wash-house, or laundry, adjoining the kitchen, but no washing machine; only a boiler, and a huge old-fashioned mangle with wooden rollers which Auntie Dorothy would turn, demonstrating formidable muscle-power. The washing was generally dried outside, and, if possible, ironed on the same day and hung to air on a rack which was suspended on ropes from the kitchen ceiling. Even though electric irons were now readily available, my aunts preferred to use the old-fashioned pair of flat-irons, heated on the kitchen range, as their mother had always done.

Auntie Myra was a fastidious house-keeper. There was, as she said, a place for everything, and everything in its place, and cleanliness was next to godliness. The kitchen floor was composed of fine red tiles which were kept scrupulously clean. Since the back door was the most-used entrance to the house, a large door-mat was provided for the thorough wiping dry of shoes before proceeding further; 'paddling' as Auntie Myra called it – i.e. marking the tiles with wet footprints – would elicit a reprimand, so in bad weather a trail of newspapers was laid from the end of the doormat to the passageway which led to the living room. A pile of old newspapers, carefully folded, was kept for this purpose in one of the cupboards, along with paper bags and other 'recyclables', in the years after the war when many things were still in short supply, and 'waste not, want not' was still a rule of life. I seem to have inherited that mentality, and will not willingly throw away anything that might possibly be re-used.

In the kitchen at Northcliff there was a large tile-clad range consisting of a fireplace, oven and hotplate. 'Doing the flues' was another of Auntie Dorothy's allotted chores, usually carried out on Friday evenings, when the range would be given a thorough going-over. Armed with a flue-brush – a sort of overgrown bottle-brush with a flexible wire handle about a metre in length – she would brush out all the accumulated soot from the chimney, then shovel out any ash from the grate-bottom, and give the whole range a thorough clean, so that the tiles gleamed, and she polished the iron-work with a graphite compound known as black lead.

It was on this range that Auntie Myra would do most of her cooking and baking. She made the most delicious cakes, and by the end of Monday afternoon, with all the washing done, she would often have done some baking too, and tea was served at the kitchen table. After tea the gramophone would sometimes come out, and at other times Auntie Myra might get out her ciné projector. Like Uncle John, she had become quite a keen amateur cinematographer in the mid-1930s and had taken lots of film on holidays and had recorded local events such as carnivals and parades. The main event of the summer was what was generally known as 'Club Day': the annual Sunday School Festival held on a Saturday in July. All the children from the various churches would process through the town with their banners, and meet in the Market Place for community hymn-singing: a colourful occasion, the Market Place being always filled to capacity with the children's groups and spectators **[21]**. Afterwards a single procession would form up, and, led by one or other of the town's bands, would head off down Stockwell Street and through the main thoroughfares. This gave the event the alternative name of 'Walking-Round Day'. The kindergarten groups would be carried on specially-decorated lorries loaned by local contractors. Several of these processions – and the sports and tea-parties which followed on various school playing fields – were carefully recorded by my aunt and uncle, along with holiday excursions to Llandudno, Southport and other seaside towns. These home movie shows were a great treat, and of course I featured on some of the films which have since passed into my own collection.

There was a small piano at Northcliff which had belonged to my grandmother who had had it specially made two octaves short in order to fit into a particular corner of the house in Dampier Street where my grandparents had lived before moving to Northcliff. I was allowed to amuse myself on this, and for a short time I had piano lessons; but although I had a musical ear I lacked either the patience or perseverence to go very far, so the lessons were discontinued. I have lived to regret this wasted opportunity.

Although Auntie Nellie and Auntie Dorothy smoked the occasional – very occasional – cigarette, perhaps at Christmas-time, Auntie Myra was the only real smoker. She habitually smoked a brand called *du Maurier,* a somewhat up-market cigarette which came in red cardboard boxes with a stylish art-deco design on the hinged lids. Auntie Myra always got the blame for introducing me to the habit, as she occasionally let me smoke the fag-end, the filter tip speared with a hat-pin as a holder. Somewhere along the line she acquired the nickname 'Nooty', and it stuck with her for the rest of her life.

Sometimes, if Auntie Myra was busy, she would suggest I might read a book, and there were plenty to choose from at Northcliff. She was quite fond of literature and poetry, and had quite a repertoire of poems which she had learned by heart. A favourite was J.G. Whittier's *Maud Muller,* which she would sometimes reel off from start to finish, with its sad ending:

'Of all sad words of tongue or pen,
The saddest are these, "It might have been".'

I have since wondered what were the 'might-have-beens' in Auntie Myra's life; why she (and indeed the other three) never married. She would have been a lovely mother, as indeed she was the most wonderful, magical aunt that anyone could have wished for, but then so were they all, in their different and equally charming ways. *Ail fam yw modryb dda* – so runs an old Welsh proverb – 'a good aunt is like a second mother', and how true. Little wonder, then, that I looked forward to the Monday visits to Northcliff, and was never ready to go home afterwards.

The Stanley Street wool shop was more than just a place of work. It was a place where friendships were made, where problems were shared, and where anyone in need would find sympathy **[22]**. Infinite care was taken to obtain what customers wanted in the way of wool and fancy goods, and even on their days off my aunts would enquire at wool shops in other areas for goods that they had not been able to obtain from their usual suppliers. Beyond the counter was a little back room into which friends might be invited for a cup of tea or coffee. I remember that clergy wives from the villages would sometimes park their husbands there – as often as not on Market Day – while they went off shopping, and the clerical gentlemen were sometimes treated to something rather stronger than tea, dispensed from a bottle concealed in the crockery cupboard.

It was on one such a day that a friend of my aunts' – Emmie, I think, was her name – swept through the shop and into the back room, in a state of high dudgeon, and plonked herself down on a chair. She had just come from the mid-week Communion at St Edward's Church.

'Well,' she exclaimed. 'He's really done it this time!'

'Who do you mean?' asked my aunt.

'Why – that new curate,' was the indignant response. 'I know he's High Church, but this morning he insisted on reading out *all* of the Ten Commandments, and – as if that wasn't enough – he told us to think about how far we had fallen short of them.'

'Did you have any particular one of them in mind?' asked my aunt, half-jokingly, but Emmie was too wound up to see the funny side.

'*Fallen short!* I'll give him fallen short! What he *should* have said was, "Think of how far you've lived up to them."'

I have sometimes used that example of self-righteous indignation to illustrate Jesus' parable of the Pharisee and the tax-collector in *Luke* chapter 18.

During the harsh Moorland winters, the shop would be heated by a paraffin stove, while in the little back room there would always be a blazing fire, with a kettle ever at the ready. Just as Auntie Myra detested wet and muddy footprints in the kitchen floor at Northcliff, Auntie Flossie did her best to keep the shop floor dry, especially when customers brought in snow on their shoes and boots. She would sometimes put down sheets of corrugated cardboard in which deliveries of wool had been packaged. Though this worked for a time, the cardboard became sodden, slid about, and looked unsightly, much to the irritation of Auntie Nellie who was heard on more than one occasion to exclaim, 'If there's any corrugated in heaven, I'm coming straight back!'

Since Auntie Myra was generally at home during the day, it was principally from her that I learned about my grandfather and other members of the Keates and Carding families. Old family photographs were sometimes brought out, and I learned exactly who was who amongst the Keateses and the Cardings. Some of the photos were of the six sisters and their young brother as children, all neatly dressed in Edwardian style. I was told how, when the seven of them walked from home to school in a morning, people would stand in admiration of this little procession of the Keates children because they were all so smartly turned out. Looking at these pictures now, I wonder just how my grandmother managed to bring up such a large family and dress them in the way she did, before the days of washing machines and other laundry aids.

Auntie Myra would sometimes talk about her father too. He appears to have been a strict disciplinarian. Mealtimes always began with Grace, and there were printed cards on the table with prayers on one side and table etiquette on the other. Both he and my grandmother had of course been born into mid-Victorian England, at a time when Charles Dickens and Anthony Trollope were still writing. I was shown some of the stories and poems that 'Grandpa Keates' had himself written and pictures he had drawn during his seven years in India as an army Reconnaissance Clerk. Many stories were told about him, for example how, for devilment, he had taken a horse through the back door of his in-laws' home – the Cardings in the Market Place – and paraded it around the kitchen table. In a more serious mood, he once gave a military-style dressing-down to Mr Samuel Scoles, headmaster of the Parish Church School, for having taken a pair of scissors to a lock of Auntie Flossie's hair which had somehow got tangled around his waistcoat button.

Whether at Northcliff or back at home, I was always happy to read, and I am grateful that there was always stimulating material available there and at school. Schoolchildren were encouraged to join the local lending library at the Nicholson Institute in Stockwell Street, so a visit to the library was another part of the weekly routine. There was a lot to choose from, and I enjoyed it all: junior fiction such as Athur Ransome's *Swallows and Amazons* and Enid Blyton's 'Adventure' books; local history, and much else. How excited I was when I saw the name 'Keats' on the spine of a book, and how disappointed when I learned that the poetry within was not my grandfather's after all. He *would* get in print, some day, I thought; and later on in life I was able to ensure that he did. The Nicholson Institute also housed a museum in the vestibule leading to the library. The walls were lined with glass-fronted cases containing exhibits and photographs relating to the history of Leek and the surrounding area, including an old iron key and a tile which had come from Dieulacres Abbey. Up the stairs leading to the art gallery on the first floor was a large window recess on which sat a display cabinet containing all kinds of treasures and caskets presented, I think, to members of the Nicholson family, while in the upper vestibule there were more display cases containing exhibits relating to the silk industry for which Leek was once famous. I remember there being quite an array of silk-moths and their cocoons. All these displays have long since been removed; in part this is a comment on changing times and the consequent need for greater security for objects of value. In their time, however, these things proved a great attraction to me, along with the library itself, opening a whole new world of adventure. Reading is, I still believe, a great liberating experience, in that it opens to young and old alike a new world in which it is possible to explore any aspect of human knowledge and experience, and to travel far.

Among the gifts that generally came my way at Christmas was the *Daily Mail Annual*, a wonderful compendium of stories, verse, features, current affairs, crossword puzzles, and things to do. It was all very well written, informative as well as entertaining; and I believe it was these books more than any others which at an early age fired my imagination and stimulated my ability to think and write.

Another favourite was *The Schoolboy's Pocket Book,* which contained a wealth of useful facts, figures, tables, weights and measures, and even the Greek alphabet which I committed to memory, and used it to exchange coded messages with other *cognoscenti.*

Although my mother and her sisters had long-established connections with St Edward's Church, their actual attendance was somewhat intermittent – certainly not every Sunday – but they prided themselves on being of the 'Old Church'. At Easter-time Auntie Dorothy would arrange the altar flowers: white arum lilies in brass vases. Dad's family had gone to All Saints', Compton, but he and his brothers had long since severed their connection following a dispute with the vicar. I used to be sent off to St Edward's Sunday School, held in the Parish Church Dayschool in Britannia Street. It was very well attended, and on occasion we would be taken up to the church for a special children's service. At around the age of nine I joined St Edward's choir, a large choir of between two and three dozen men and boys **[23]**. I seemed to have a modest talent for singing, and there were other attractions too in the form of choir outings and a small remuneration paid every quarter according to attendance at the two Sunday services and at choir practice. It averaged out, as I remember, at about £1 per year, but in those days £1 would go a long way when a bag of sweets (or chips), or a copy of the *Beano*, could be bought for sixpence (2½p), and £1 would buy several gramophone records. Extra remuneration was given for attendance and weddings and funerals, of which there were quite a number each year, and there were the annual coach-trips too.

On joining the choir, a new boy would be kitted out with a cassock and 'sausage-skin' surplice, allotted a peg in the choir vestry, and also be given a number preceded by either the letter C or the letter D to indicate the side of the choir where you would sit. The classification C and D originates in cathedral choirs, D (short for Decani) signifying the stalls on the south side of the chancel where the Dean (*Decanus*) sits, and C (short for Cantoris) indicating those on the north side where the Precentor (*Cantor*) has his stall; not really applicable to a parish church which has neither dean nor precentor, but the practice became widespread in church choirs. I was allocated C5. Joining the choir also involved an unofficial rite of initiation presided over by the senior boy choristers. In the churchyard, just below the east window there was a large table-tomb, and in front of it was a bush – a yew as I remember. Any new boy was required to stand on the tomb and jump into the middle of the bush. If he refused, two senior boys would take him by the arms and legs, and throw him in. Wisely, I agreed to jump, and emerged with only one or two minor scratches. Choir practices were held on Friday evenings, and were generally followed by some of us visiting the West End chip shop on the way home. Eating in the street was in those days frowned upon, and perhaps quite rightly so in view of the current widespread habit of 'grazing', so we sometimes took to the shelter in Westwood Recreation ground, and consumed our chips there.

Shortly after I joined the choir, the organ underwent a complete restoration and rebuild. It was housed in what had originally been intended as a side-chapel at the east end of the south aisle, completely blocking the east window of what was now generally referred to as 'the organ chamber', and separated from the chancel by a pair of arches and wrought-iron screenwork, all of which obscured the sight-line between the organist and the choir. During the restoration, a Hammond organ provided the accompaniment for choir and congregation. At around the same time the appearance of the nave was changed through the removal of the side-galleries which had been installed in Georgian times.

One of the highlights of the year for us choirboys was to climb to the top of the church tower each Trinity Sunday before the main service, to sing a couple of Trinity hymns. Clad in their cassocks and surplices, men and boys would ascend the spiral staircase catching ever-widening views of the town below through the small windows. The staircase took us past the opening into the bell-chamber. The sight of ten heavy bells revolving on their frames was awesome and the sound of them was deafening. Finally we emerged on to the parapet from where we would take in the whole panorama of the town and the surrounding countryside. To the west lay the Cheshire plain, to the north and east the Staffordshire uplands with their rugged outcrops of millstone grit, with the sun glinting on the windows of cars as they toiled uphill towards Buxton. Over to the south lay the outer edges of the Potteries towns. People would assemble in the street below and look upwards, but what they could hear of our singing was anyone's guess. Then, after one final taking-in of the view, we would hurry down the staircase, hoping to get past the bell-chamber before the ringers started up again.

Choir practice was held in church on Friday evenings. We rehearsed the hymns for the following Sunday's services, and particular attention was given to the pointing of psalms and canticles as well as to the various chants. Anthems were often included at evensong, and these were introduced and practised for several weeks ahead of the performance date. There were some extra services too, as St Edward's was very much the 'civic' church of the town. Remembrance Sunday was one such, with an additional service in the afternoon, and a big procession through the town to 'the Monument' for the wreath-laying. Christmas brought its round of carol services, including – naturally – the one with the Nine Lessons. I remember a Nativity play, in which it was decided that real incense would be used at the entrance of the Three Kings with their gifts. I was chosen to be Caspar's attendant, and to walk in front of him dressed – anachronistically – in my choir robes, swinging a smoking thurible which had been borrowed for the occasion from a church in the Potteries. This was, I guess, the first time that incense had been burned in St Edward's since the 1550s.

Choir outings generally took us to the seaside, to Blackpool, Llandudno, New Brighton, and also to Chester Zoo. Choirmen's wives would usually come along, and also the organist, Miss Ada Parr, then around fifty years old, or so it seemed to us youngsters. On the morning of an outing to Blackpool she failed to appear in the Market Place from where the bus would start, and after waiting for a time it was concluded that she wasn't coming, and so the bus set off. As we travelled down Church Street, the figure of Ada appeared, running like mad and frantically waving her handbag and umbrella. She had overslept. That was not the only incident of the day. While at Blackpool we all visited the Pleasure Beach, and while in the Fun House, Ada – who had a playful side to her nature – decided to have a go on the giant slide. We all stood and watched open-mouthed as she climbed the steps and stood at the top of the slide. Then, whoosh! Down she came, but as she did so, her ample skirt flew up right over her head, revealing what a sniggering choirman described as 'all the colours of the rainbow.'

In 1952 the Vicar of St Edward's, the Revd. Norman Watson, retired. His farewell address consisted of an account of the history of Leek, the parish church and the abbey of Dieulacres, drawn from his own extensive researches. I found it fascinating, and this, more than any other single thing, fired my interest in local history, impelling me to find out more. It was around this time too that I was taken on a summer outing to Alton village. We went by train from Leek, down the Churnet Valley to Oakamoor, then walked through Dimmingsdale into the lower part of Alton, dominated by the castle perched high up on the edge of a cliff overlooking the River Churnet. Later in the day I was taken into the castle precincts, to look at the adjacent convent buildings, and the little church of St John's. I shall never forget that experience. It was like entering another world, which is indeed what it is: the world of A.W.N. Pugin and the nineteenth-century Gothic Revival, although in those days I knew nothing of them; but it was a world of spires and pinnacles, glowing stained glass and twinkling candles, like nothing I had ever seen before; and outside the sun was shining on the coloured tiles of the roof of the castle chapel. Auntie Flossie was with us on that day. She would never go into a church with her head uncovered, and so, being hatless on that warm summer's afternoon, she took a small lace-edged handkerchief out of her handbag, and put in on her head like a diminutive *mantilla*, which I thought was very funny. Though not herself a Catholic, she showed me how to use the holy water in the stoup by the door, and we lit votive candles in front of the statue of St Joseph. That, I suppose, was my first introduction to the religion, as well as the buildings, of Pugin and the sixteenth Earl of Shrewsbury, and the day when I began – unconsciously no doubt – to incline towards Catholicism.

My father was a keen fisherman, and a member of a local angling club. In his younger days he had played cricket, mainly at Highfields Cricket Club, had taken part in competitions, and had won a few trophies. Mother's game had been tennis, and she too had taken part competitively. At the time of their marriage they both agreed to give up their sports, something which they later regretted. Fishing was now a more sedate alternative, and fishing trips took us to various places including Froghall, on the Cauldon canal, where we would go by train down the Churnet Valley line. It was on one such fishing trip that I first saw Alton Towers, the former home of the Talbot earls of Shrewsbury, now run by a local businessman named Dennis Bagshaw. Having been closed during the war years, the Towers opened again to the public in 1952. There were then none of the theme-park rides which have since made Alton Towers famous: only the gardens and the big lake in front of the great house which was at this time derelict, the owner having removed lead from the roofs and stripped out the timber and furnishings in order to pay off a bank loan; so perished one of the grandest Gothic interiors in the whole of England. It was possible to obtain a fishing permit for the lake, so Dad and I went one day with some of his fishing friends, and sat by the lake on the opposite side to the house. Few fish were caught, as I remember, but the Gothic mansion across the water exerted a great pull, with its battlements, towers and pinnacles.

We returned another day to look round the gardens and the outside of the house, where I had my photograph taken in front of the big window of the Octagon, on the south side of the mansion **[25]**. Little did I imagine then that Alton and the Towers would come to occupy an important part of my subsequent career as an historian, but these early experiences have never been forgotten.

Though I would sometimes go fishing with my father, and had my own rod and line, I never became an enthusiast. Sitting for hours at the side of a canal watching for the float to bob under the water was not the most exciting way to spend a Saturday afternoon, although it did offer the opportunity for quiet reflection and day-dreaming. Mother would sometimes come along, having prepared a picnic for us all to share. More often she would stay at home, and have an enamel plate ready to receive the 'catch of the day', more in hope than certainty, although there were occasional surprises. After one such expedition, Dad opened his fishing basket and took out a large freshwater fish, wrapped in a damp cloth. It was duly transferred to the plate which was put into the cold oven to keep it fresh until the next day, as we had no fridge. Later that evening a strange flapping and rattling sound was heard to come from the oven, and Mum went to investigate. She opened the door to find that the trout had somehow revived, and was jumping about inside the oven. Mother was not amused. Moreover, her oven was often used for the drying of stale bread begged from the corner shop, which Dad would then turn into ground-bait using Mum's mincing machine. 'Fishing,' she would sometimes say, 'is a piece of string with a maggot on one end and a fool on the other.'

Maggots were the favourite live bait, kept in an aluminium tin with a gauze panel in the top for ventilation. One of my regular errands was to get this tin filled by taking it to a maggot breeder in Kiln Lane. He kept his stock of maggots in sawdust-filled buckets in the outside toilet at the back of his cottage. You could cut the smell with a knife. One Saturday evening, Dad returned from his fishing trip, dumped his rod and basket in the hall, and went off to join his friends at the local, leaving Mum and I listening to the radio in the living room. About an hour later, Mum let out a shriek and pointed to the carpet by the door. A swarm of maggots was advancing across the carpet, having wriggled under the door, and there were more maggots on the loose in the hall. It appeared that the maggot tin had up-ended in the basket, the lid had come off, and the contents were escaping through the wickerwork. It took ages to clear them all away, and the expression, 'Wait till your father gets home,' took on a whole new meaning.

So far I have said little about my friends of those days. There were the children of the immediate neighbourhood in Sneyd Avenue, such as Arthur and Elizabeth Massey, Sylvia Rowlands, and Barry Hollinshead. Barry followed me into St Edward's choir, where many other friendships were formed. In addition to the choir outings we sometimes went to sing in Lichfield Cathedral, and in the Victoria Hall, Hanley, at the annual Festival of Remembrance in November. There were the many friends I made at school, and among the special ones were Martin Knowles, whose father kept a butcher's shop in West Street, and his mother opened a flower shop in Westwood Road. Martin was just a day older than me, so his birthday was easily remembered. Eventually he entered the family business, and later moved to Shropshire. Then there was Cameron Watson whose father had a medical practice in Stockwell Street; a huge three-storey house with attics and cellars, a place to let the imagination run riot. The 'brains' of our class at Westwood Road was David Murfin who eventually went on to read Physics at Cambridge, and was later ordained as a Methodist minister. It was, of course, a mixed infant/junior school, and I can remember many of the girls, such as Angela Whalley, Vivienne Emmott, Margaret Crump, Joan Clowes; and Heather, the girl with whom, at the age of nine, I fell in love. She was a tall girl with beautiful eyes. I remember sitting next to her at one of the school Christmas parties. She was wearing a pretty smocked dress, and a 'bunny-wool' cardigan. Then there was Anne, a new girl to the school. I thought she was very pretty too, but I was seen off by my arch-rival for her affections, and I remember how wretched I felt!

As my mother and aunts had all been born either in the last five years of the nineteenth century or the first five years of the twentieth, they had been brought up in accordance with the Victorian/ Edwardian values of the time. My mother told me that family meals had always begun with the Grace said, up until his illness and death in 1917, by my grandfather. There was a strict code of table-manners. It was generally understood, for example, that whether in a restaurant or at home, nobody would begin to eat until everybody had been served; just plain good manners, really. Conservative both in nature and politics, staunchly royalist and extremely patriotic, 'the girls' had all been members of the 'Junior Imps' (the precursor of the Young Conservatives), and some had been involved with the League of Empire Loyalists, and the Primrose League. My mother, coincidentally, had been born on Primrose Day, 19th April, and was often called 'Primrose' by my grandmother. Primrose Day was, in Conservative circles, an annual celebration of the great Conservative Prime Minister, Benjamin Disraeli to whom, famously, Queen Victoria had once sent a gift of primroses. The importance of good manners and politeness was instilled into me both at home and at school. I was taught, for example, always to stand up when a lady entered the room, always to give up my seat to a lady on a bus or train, and to raise my hat when greeting a lady outdoors, until they became second nature to me, as indeed they still are, whatever the so-called 'politically correct' brigade might have to say about such niceties. Opening a door to allow a lady to go through first, and walking on the outside when out in the street are simply acts of courtesy, and it seems to me more than a pity that we have largely lost them through neglect and ignorance.

On February 6th 1952 King George VI died. He had been ill for some time following an operation for lung cancer, and he looked terribly ill at the time of his last public appearance a few days previously when he had said farewell to his daughter, Princess Elizabeth, and the Duke of Edinburgh, as they flew off on an official visit to Kenya. The farewell turned out to be a goodbye, and the nation was plunged into mourning. Regular radio and television broadcasts were suspended, and solemn music was played over the air instead. Local memorial services were held, including the one at St Edward's Church, which all the pupils and staff at Westwood Road attended. The country came to a halt on the day of the funeral, and the newspapers were full of pictures of the funeral procession to Westminster Abbey, and the subsequent journey to Windsor where the King was buried.

Mourning later gave way to the excitement of the accession of Elizabeth II, and the prospect of a coronation, but before that came around, I had my first experience of hospital. As a child I had enjoyed reasonably good health, apart from the usual childhood illnesses which everyone had; but even as a baby I had trouble with my ears, and if ever I caught a cold, it would almost inevitably lead to a bout of very painful earache. Following a walk over Hillswood on a cold and windy day (I remember quite clearly that it was March 1st – St David's Day), I had a particularly severe attack of earache, and this time the doctor referred me to an ear, nose and throat specialist at the North Staffs Hospital. A few weeks later I was in Longton Cottage Hospital having adenoids removed, and another small operation to clear the eustachian tubes. I was in there for just about a week, during which time no visitors were allowed. It was hospital policy not to allow children to be visited by parents or other relatives 'for fear of unsettling them'. Nowadays, when parents are allowed to visit freely and even to stay overnight, such regulations appear almost barbaric. The good thing was that I have never had earache since.

The Queen's coronation took place on 2nd June 1953. Leek, like all other towns and villages, was festooned with decorations. Even the kerb-stones of the pavements were painted in red, white and blue, triumphal arches were built over the main roads at the entrances to the town, and some of the smaller streets followed suit. At Sneyd Avenue we strung up bunting and flags between the houses, and Dad built a special display in the front-room window, the main feature of which was an illuminated sailing-ship which he had made. The hull was carved from wood, and the sails made from folded parchment with electric bulbs inside. This was placed on a wooden box draped with the Union Flag. He also framed up a large portrait of the Queen and made a gold-painted easel to stand it on. These formed part of a display which my aunts created in the shop window as their entry in the window-dressing competition organised by the local Chamber of Trade **[25]**. They won first prize. To mark the coronation the Chamber of Trade also arranged for a plantation of trees on the summit of Hillswood, that favourite spot of mine, and a commemorative plaque was built into the boundary wall. When the celebrations were over, the Queen's portrait was taken from the shop down to Northcliff, where it hung on the kitchen wall for the next thirty years or more.

On Coronation Day itself we all went to Lowther Place and huddled round Auntie Mary and Uncle John's television set to watch the procession and the coronation service, which seemed to last a very long time. One of the most popular figures in the procession was Queen Salote of Tonga, who insisted on keeping the top of her carriage open in the pouring rain which somewhat marred the day, and smiling broadly at the crowds. Later in the evening we all went down to the Birchall Playing Fields where there was a huge firework display. There was also an ox-roast in the Market Place. By the time we arrived the ox had all been eaten and we queued in vain!

As an end-of-term treat in the summer of 1953 a train excursion to Windsor was arranged for the top classes at Westwood Road, and parents were invited too. We had a tour of Windsor Castle, and a boat-trip on the Thames to Runnymede to see where Magna Carta had been granted by King John in 1215.

Coronation year was memorable for Auntie Mary and Uncle John in that in 1953 Uncle John was elected President of his professional body, the North Staffs. branch of the Pharmaceutical Society of Great Britain. They were already committee members, but now they found themselves invited to a wide range of social engagements in the county, which Auntie Mary particularly enjoyed, and which involved Uncle John in much additional expenditure on new dresses for her. They also had an extension built on to the house, to help cope with all the entertaining.

In the autumn of 1953 I began my last year at Westwood Road School, and there was the need to focus on the eleven-plus examination which would determine which school I would go to in the following September. I don't remember having any particular anxiety about the exam, which we sat not in our own school but in the Britannia Street Secondary Modern School which was one of the two schools available to those who did not obtain a place at grammar school.

In the September of 1953 I had my first experience of a death within the family when Granddad Fisher died at the age of seventy-five after several months' illness. I remember him as a kindly old gentleman with white wavy hair, whom I used to visit at least once a week. The funeral took place at All Saints', the church which my father's family had attended until he and his brothers left after a disagreement with the parish priest. It had been agreed among the family that the grandsons would not attend the funeral, in case we might find the experience 'upsetting'. In later life I have, as a priest, conducted funeral services at which quite young children have been present, and to me it seems the most natural thing in the world that they should be there. I find that young people will often accept the fact of death much more readily than many adults, and I believe that excluding children from these rites of passage is mistaken, having much more to do with adults projecting their own fears and hang-ups quite unnecessarily on to the children. What I do remember most clearly is that in September 1953 I felt both hurt and resentful at not being allowed to go to my grandfather's funeral, the more especially because, as a chorister at St Edward's, I often sang at the funerals of complete strangers.

The Christmas of 1953 was the last we spent at 7 Sneyd Avenue. Moving house, changing schools, coping with adolescence – these were just a few of the things on the horizon which signalled the end of the childhood years. Looking back now on those first ten years of my life, I realise how fortunate I was to have been brought up in that environment, and with so much around me that was challenging, stimulating, and seminal too in that interests were kindled which grew and blossomed in later life. Childhood was precisely that, with no pressures to grow up before it was time, and with few of the dangers and corrupt influences which have come to surround later generations. Sometimes, on a winter's day when it goes dark early, and the local children come out of school, my mind goes back to those early days in Leek; how, for example, I would walk from Westwood Road School on such a day, just as the gas-lamps were turned on. On my way along West Street I might call into the pharmacy and have a chat with Uncle John; or if it was a Monday there would be tea and home-made cakes at Auntie Myra's. Or I might go up into the town, where the shop-windows were lit up and decorated for Christmas, and the paper boy on the corner called out, 'Sentinel!' In the little wool shop in Stanley Street the faint smell of paraffin from the old-fashioned stove which kept the customers warm in winter would mingle with the smells of wool and fabrics; then, in the back room, the aroma of tea and toast and melted butter in front of the open fire; Auntie Dorothy sitting in her corner knitting socks, Auntie Flossie with her toasting fork, and Auntie Nellie in the shop dealing with a late customer. On such days I am enveloped once more in the warm glow of childhood, and I say, 'Thanks for the memory'.

3

FINDING MY FEET: THE JOYS AND PAINS OF ADOLESCENCE

In the spring of 1954 we moved from 7 Sneyd Avenue, which was, as I have said, rented from a private landlord, who at this time wished to move into the house himself following his retirement. Buying a house was not a viable option at this time, although my father had already moved from the Sneyd Engineering Works to a better-paid job at the engineering firm of F. Bode, on the Buxton Road. So we went into another rented house, the owner of which lived in Blackpool and was unlikely to return to Leek – or so we thought at the time. The house was called 'Langford', no. 5 Spring Gardens, at the west end of the town and nearer to Westwood Road School. Like the house at Sneyd Avenue, it was on a corner, but there was, alas, no big garden at the side; only a small one at the back, and an even smaller one at the front, just a patch of grass, and a privet hedge. To compensate, however, there was the Westwood Recreation Ground just across the road, and beyond the 'Rec' was Westwood Road where my great-aunt Myra lived. We quickly settled in, and my mother was happier at Spring Gardens than in any other home we lived in. We had excellent neighbours – Bill and Annie Moss – at no. 3. Mrs Moss and my mother became good friends, while my father found a firm friend and fishing companion in Spencer Clowes, Annie's brother. Spencer's two children, Joan and Pamela, were already known to me as they went to Westwood Road School. On the opposite corner of Spring Gardens and Langford Street lived the Mitchell family. Mr Mitchell taught chemistry at Leek High School, and his son, Philip, sang in St Edward's church choir.

In the summer of 1954 Great-aunt Myra ('Auntie-Auntie') died at the age of eighty. She had lived at the Carding family house in Westwood Road with a companion, Miss Frances Cooke, whom we called Auntie Fanny. She was in fact related by marriage, being the sister of John Cooke who had married another of my grandmother's younger sisters, Eliza Carding. My aunties Myra and Flossie had been particularly kind to 'Auntie-Auntie', helping to look after her during her illness. The funeral, as I remember, was a somewhat grand affair, in the tradition of the Cardings, with a packed church and a sea of floral tributes, and there was no question of my not attending as I was required in any case to sing with the choir. Although great-aunt Myra had never married, there were lots of nephews and nieces, including my mother and her five sisters, and the proceeds of the sale of the house and contents were divided amongst them. There was some fine furniture in the house, which had changed very little over the decades, and a few nice Victorian/Edwardian pieces came our way.

Meanwhile I had sat the eleven-plus examination, and was selected for grammar school. There were several possibilities: Leek High School, which was within walking distance, or one of the more distant ones such as Newcastle High School, Hanley

High School, or Wolstanton Grammar. There was a good deal of parental choice. Cameron Watson's parents chose to send him to Wolstanton (which he habitually referred to as 'The Dungeon'), while Philip Mitchell went to Newcastle. Both of these schools opened on Saturday mornings, with Wednesday afternoons off to compensate. My own preference was for Leek High, so I started there in September 1954. Situated on the opposite side of the road to Westwood Primary School, it was built in similar style, but around a central quadrangle; and it stood in spacious landscaped grounds, with big playing-fields running eastwards from the school buildings to the boundary of the Westwood Recreation Ground. To an eleven-year-old, everything seemed larger than life.

Several of my friends from Westwood Road went on to the high school too – Martin Knowles, Vernon Turner, David Murfin, Alan Machin – but there were many new faces from other Leek schools, and then there were the 'bus boys' who came in from places such as Cheddleton, Cheadle, Endon and Brown Edge. Alas, none of my former playmates from Sneyd Avenue made it to the High School, though I still saw them from time to time, especially Arthur and Elizabeth Massey.

Leek High School had been built in the 1930s in similar style to Westwood Road Primary school, but of course it was much larger. It was a boys-only establishment. Most of the girls who passed the eleven-plus went to the girls' high school at Westwood Hall, half a mile or so further on from the boys' high school, and most definitely off-limits to the boys. It was an all-male staff at LHS too; the masters wore their black academic gowns, and another novelty was that instead of staying in one classroom for all the lessons, we moved around, especially for subjects like science, geography and art, which had their specialist rooms. Another big difference was that instead of being called by our Christian names, as we were in junior school, we were now called by surname only.

Added to this was a permanent number which appeared on all relevant school documents such as end-of-term reports, and on the front of exercise-books along with one's name. So for the next few years I was known as 'No. 157 Fisher'. Another curious thing was that we were all weighed and measured by the P.E. master at the end of each term, so that height and weight could be entered on our reports. Uniform consisted of cap, maroon blazer with the letters LHS woven on the breast pocket, and grey flannel shorts **[26]**. Short trousers were *de rigueur* for first- and second-year boys. It's hard to imagine today's thirteen-year-olds being forced into flannel shorts, but that's the way it was.

Leek High School was a two-form entry establishment, the forms being designated as IIA and II Alpha, the A/Alpha designation continuing through to the Fifth Year. They were parallel in terms of pupils' abilities. I think I can still remember the Form Roll as it was called out at morning and afternoon registration:

> Ball, Barr, Beech, Betteley, Cliff, Cooper, Fisher, Gaskell, Hampson, Harrison, Heathcote, Hindley, Jones, Knowles, Machin, Maycock, Mycock, Owen, Pakeman, Reeves, Rushton B.A., Rushton J., Salt, Skelding, Smith, Sneyd, Turner, White, Williams, Woodward.

I can still picture them in my mind's eye: thirty of us in all, to which a thirty-first was added somewhat later, with the arrival of Edward Alcock, a cousin of Alan Machin, whose family had moved to Leek from Northern Ireland. The first two names on the roll were now Alcock and Ball, which caused considerable amusement amongst the boys, and, I have no doubt, in the staff-room too.

The school had its own unofficial initiation rite. New boys were as likely as not to be 'ducked', i.e. taken by older boys to the wash-room next to the toilets, and have their heads held under the drinking-water tap. This would go on for several days at the start of each new intake; any who managed to avoid a ducking were generally safe after the first week.

The atmosphere of the school was highly competitive. One aspect of this was the system of 'tri-weeklies' in which marks gained in each subject over the three-week period were grossed up, and pupils listed in their overall position in class from 1 to 31. An individual's progress over the term was then assessed by examining his up-and-down movements, and the tri-weekly results were entered on the end-of-term report to parents. Homework to a set timetable was also a new experience, so studies continued into the evening, and at weekends too, with homework exercises collected in and marked, and punishments imposed upon defaulters.

Calling by name and number was just one aspect of the regimental lines upon which the school was run in those days. Morning assembly was dismissed in military fashion. After the headmaster had left the hall, the second master would take command. 'School, atten-shun!', he would shout; 'Outwards turn!', 'Stand at ease!'. It took some getting used to, especially after the gentler regime at Westwood Road Primary School.

Get used to it I did, however, and I found all the new subjects interesting; science, history and geography taught for the first time as separate subjects, and French which I particularly enjoyed. Maths was a struggle. I had never excelled at arithmetic, but had done well enough at it to pass the eleven-plus; Geometry I positively enjoyed, but algebra and calculus were mysteries which I never fully fathomed, and this weakness dogged me right through to the 'O' level exam, and spoiled my chances of pursuing a scientific career which was something that I seriously considered.

All written work was done with pen and ink, and pencil. Ball-point pens were forbidden, and pupils in the lower school were not allowed to bring fountain pens. Instead we had to use the dip-in variety provided by the school, and each desk was equipped with an ink well. These had to be filled periodically from a metal container shaped a bit like a miniature watering-can with a long spout. Members of the class took it in turn to be ink monitor, which meant checking that the ink wells were topped up, and, when supplies ran out, mixing ink powder with water to make a fresh supply. Needless to say, the time-honoured practice of flicking ink-soaked paper pellets with a ruler was not unknown to us! The quality of paper in the various exercise books was not very good: rough in texture and difficult to write on with the dip-in pens, the pointed nibs of which sometimes went right through the paper. Writing had of course to be joined-up, and we had begun to learn this in the final year at junior school. Whether or not because of the quality of the paper and pens, my handwriting was not good, and I well remember the geography master, Mr Chapman, looking over my shoulder one day and saying, 'Write in English, Fisher, not in Hindu!' I took the hint, and resolved there and then to do something about it. Amongst my aunts' friends and acquaintances was Frederick Tunnicliffe, the wholesaler from whom they purchased most of their stock, and he was a frequent visitor to the wool shop. He had a most beautiful handwriting style, cursive and verging on copperplate. I took that as my model and began to practise. My mother's handwriting was also clear and even, though backward-sloping as her father's had been. I also acquired a decent fountain pen which I was of course free to use at home. From that day to this I have always preferred to use an ink-pen. Ball-points are handy, but they are less easy to control, and it is impossible to obtain the alternate thick and thin strokes that are essential in forming letters of the copperplate type, which was my chosen model. I later went on to study different calligraphic styles, and, years later, to practise chisel-cut lettering on slate and stone. Thus the geography teacher's sarcastic remark produced long-term results.

The headmaster, Mr L.G. Ramsay, was a remote figure whom we generally saw only at morning assembly. His study lay through the 'Crush Hall' a dimly-lit oak-panelled vestibule adjoining the assembly hall, with its own private entrance reserved for the head and the secretary, Miss Jean Goodwin. Most of the masters had nicknames. The second master, Mr Parrack, was known as 'Tusky' on account of his walrus-like moustache. The French master, Mr Lazarus was known either as 'Sol' (his first name being Solomon), or 'Vulture' because of his piercing bespectacled eyes, hooked nose, stooping gait, and the black gown which more often than not had slipped half-way down his back and trailed on the floor behind him. There was D.N.Jones, the woodwork master, known as 'Dizzy' because of his bland expression, but we soon discovered that he was not as 'dizzy' as he looked, and was in fact a fierce disciplinarian with a strong Welsh accent. Stern warnings to would-be miscreants often ended with a scriptural quote in which we would all join in chorus, 'There will be much weeping and wailing and gnashing of teeth'!

Dizzy's department was known as the M.I. Room. M.I. signified 'Manual Instruction' and it covered different handicrafts including woodwork, metalwork and pottery. In the first term we did pottery, making a variety of items out of grey clay which was scooped out of a large tub. Although there was a pottery kiln in an alcove just outside the M.I. Room, none of our pieces was ever fired. At the end of each class we were required to deposit our creations back in the clay-bin, to be pounded up ready for the next class. It all seemed a waste of effort.

Moving on to woodwork, we were taught how to make mortise-and-tenon joints, and dovetails, and we actually made pieces to take home, for example a table-lamp and a book-shelf. The one permanent souvenir I have of those days is a scar on the middle finger of my right hand, sustained when – foolishly – I held a piece of timber steady while another boy attacked it with a chisel. The chisel slipped, lacerating my finger to the bone, and there was blood everywhere. Fortunately there was a visiting doctor on the premises. He took me in his car up to the surgery, stitched and dressed the wound, and then drove me back to school.

Punishments meted out by masters varied. The giving of 'lines' was still a common practice as a corrective, involving the writing out of a sentence or phrase fifty or a hundred times. After making some elementary mistake in an algebra lesson, I was told to write, 'When you divide, you subtract the powers', fifty times. It was a chore, but the lesson was learned! Detention after school on Tuesdays and Fridays was meted out for more serious offences, and it was accompanied by a set ritual in which the master would send the offending boy to the staff-room to collect the big red detention register into which name and number would be inscribed. The list of detainees would be read aloud in morning assembly, and the number of detentions would be recorded on the end-of-term report. The school prefects also had authority to hand out impositions, and these were recorded in the separate Prefects' Punishment Book, usually referred to by the boys as 'Tot'. Corporal punishment by caning was used sparingly, as I remember, as the ultimate deterrent, and administered only by the headmaster in his study, always witnessed by another member of staff, and duly recorded in a special punishment book.

'Tiny' Baines, the maths master was anything but tiny, and he also conducted the school choir. There was the geography master, Jack Chapman, nicknamed 'Penguin' because of his rotund figure, plastered-down black hair, and waddling gait. Alwynne Walmesley, known to the boys as 'Wigwam', was our history master; a kindly man, and a practising Quaker as I discovered later. He it was who further enthused me about the past with his dramatic accounts of Edward I's campaigns in Scotland and Wales. I remember a story he told about a train journey to Scotland. Sitting opposite him was a kilted Scotsman who had absolutely nothing to say until the train pulled in to a small station north of the border. 'Bannockburn!' exclaimed the Scotsman, as if to say, 'That's where we beat ye', and then lapsed once more into silence.

The 'House' system was one of many features of the public boarding-schools which were adapted by the grammar schools, and mainly for competitive sporting purposes. There were four such houses at LHS: Hall, Milner and Nicholson, named after three of the school's benefactors, and Warrington, named after a former headmaster. Organised games played an important part in the life of the school. We were introduced to rugby in the first term, hockey in the second, and then in the third term there was cricket. I endured rugby, but never really enjoyed it; and football was banned. I quite liked hockey, also cricket which D.N. Jones (a keen rugby man) dismissed as 'a game of statues'. It soon became clear, however, that I was not going to become good enough at any of it to get into school teams, and probably through my own lack of effort and enthusiasm. D.N. Jones, who assisted with rugby, spotted that there was some potential. On one occasion he made me stand on the touch-line between the goal-posts, and lined up all the others on the opposing three-quarter line. He then gave me the ball, and told me that I was to run with it towards the opposite touch-line, and all the others would try to stop me. If I did not get beyond the centre-line I would get a detention. I was not a bad runner, and I remember getting well beyond the line before I was brought down. It may have been a rather cruel thing for 'Dizzy' Jones to have done, but he proved a point: I *could* run with the ball and fight off opposition if I set my mind to it. Neverthless, I would make any excuse to dodge the games field, especially in winter. Why should I have to endure the rain and the mud and the cold when my time could be spent more profitably in a warm and comfortable library?

There was a range of clubs and societies which met after school, and I joined some of these; for example the Geographical Society. Visiting speakers came to talk about travels in different parts of the world, often illustrated with films and slides. There was the *Cercle Francais* presided over by Mr Lazarus. Conversation in French was encouraged, and we learned a number of French songs.

Music formed a part of the curriculum in the first year, when singing was timetabled for one afternoon per week. The sessions would take place in the assembly hall, with Mr Baines directing, and Mr Chapman at the piano. The repertoire we learned included 'Linden Lea', the Soldiers' Chorus from *Faust,* and – inevitably – 'Nymphs and Shepherds'. We were also taught the descant line to the *Crimond* setting of the 23rd Psalm, 'The Lord's my Shepherd', so that we could perform it whenever that hymn occurred in morning assembly. Boys with decent voices were drafted into the school choir, which always performed one or two songs at the annual 'Speech Day', when the school prizes and trophies were presented, usually by some distinguished guest; also the 'O' and 'A' level certificates. Thus it was the single most important event in the school calendar, when the boys were expected to turn out super-clean and tidy, and when the masters wore full academic dress, i.e. both gown and hood, which was something of a surprise, for until then I had seen academic hoods only on the backs of clergymen in church, not realising that they signified a university degree and therefore not specifically 'clerical'. The prize-giving was presided over by the Chairman of the Board of Governors, a Dr Alkins, resplendent in his red-and-cream doctor's robes.

Morning assemblies, as I have already hinted, were quite regimented affairs. The headmaster would lead the formal prayers, and there would always be a hymn, accompanied by piano and other instruments such as cello, oboe, cornet and trombone. Any boy who was proficient on an instrument was liable to be drafted in. Every year there was a dramatic or musical production to which the paying public were invited. In my first year it was to be Benjamin Britten's *Let's Make an Opera/The Little Sweep.* There was an element of audience participation, and so we were taught the relevant songs so as to be able to give a lead on performance nights. Mr Baines, naturally, was the producer, and the acting roles were taken by a mixed cast of pupils and staff.

In the summer of 1955 we went on what was easily the most memorable family holiday of all: a fortnight in Criccieth. I suspect that it was Auntie-Auntie's legacy which made such a holiday possible, and it was one which I still look back to with very happy memories of what was to be the last childhood holiday by the sea. I don't know quite why Criccieth was chosen. We had never been to that part of Wales before; but I think the prospect of a little sea-fishing and angling in the River Dwyfor attracted my father. So, one Saturday morning we set off for Leek station, laden with our luggage which included Dad's fishing tackle, and Nell the dog. It was more or less a whole day's journey: first to Stoke, then via Chester and Llandudno Junction, and yet another change of train which eventually took us along the coastal line to Criccieth. We stayed at the Windsor Guest House, on the Marine Terrace west of the castle. I fell in love instantly with Criccieth and the surrounding area. We were blessed with glorious weather for the whole fortnight, and as well as spending time on the beach, we had outings to Porthmadog, Black Rock, and a ride on the narrow-gauge Ffestiniog Railway which had just been partly reopened. We also walked to the neighbouring village of Llanystumdwy, to see the grave of David Lloyd George, at the side of the river Dwyfor. There were fishing-trips too; the most memorable being in a rowing-boat which Dad hired for the day. We set off from the jetty by the castle, and headed west. Few fish were caught, but there were spectacular views, and Nell didn't seem to mind the boat too much. Then I noticed a line of buoys marking the position of lobster pots. They appeared to be moving; then I realised that it wasn't the buoys that were moving, but our boat. We had got caught in a tide-slick close to the Dwyfor estuary. Dad realised at once that we were running into trouble, so he seized the oars and rowed as hard as he could to get us out of the current. It took a long time to get us back to land; a narrow escape, and an experience that we had no wish to repeat.

As the holiday drew to a close I wished that we could stay longer, or that Dad could get a job locally so that we could move to Criccieth. He did in fact consider a job on offer at the Trawsfynydd Nuclear Power Station, but concluded that, considering its remoteness, it might not be such a good move. Before we left Criccieth I scratched my initials and the date on a small fragment of slate which I had picked up from the beach. I hid it in a secret place near the flag-pole on Dinas hill, just opposite Criccieth Castle. It was a boyish way of saying that I was leaving a part of me in Criccieth, and that one day I would return. It was to be another fifteen years before I saw Criccieth again, by which time I had a wife, and a child of my own.

Except when on holiday, eating out was a rare treat. 'Pub meals' didn't yet exist, and fish-and-chip shops were the only fast-food outlets, apart from the bakeries such as Maskerys in St Edward Street, and Brassingtons in Garden Street, near to my aunts' house. Maskerys made a range of delicious pies, and they also held the secret recipe for Leek gingerbread. This delicacy consisted of flat cakes of gingerbread, cut into fingers like thick biscuits, and packed in cardboard boxes. Leek had a few cafés: Tatton's in Derby Street has already been mentioned; then there was Howarth's 'White Hart' tea rooms at the top of Stockwell Street, and some smaller tea-shops. There were a few hotels, such as the Red Lion in the Market Place, the Swan at the top of St Edward Street, and the Three Horseshoes at Blackshaw Moor catered for those with their own transport. Signs of change came with the opening of Leek's first Chinese restaurant, the Kan Wah, in the Market Place, although many people treated it with suspicion to begin with, and there were dark rumours as to what the chop suey might actually have contained. More exotic foods began to appear in grocers' shops, such as the 'Vesta' range of dehydrated Chinese and Indian dishes for home preparation, and packets of chicken noodle soup, again in dried form. I remember Dad turning up his nose at this, and saying that the only noodles were the folks who ate such rubbish!

On returning to school in September 1955, we all began a second foreign language, either Latin or German. The selection, it seems, was quite arbitrary, and the boys had no say in it whatsoever. I was put into the Latin set, and since I had no particular preference, I did not mind. I quite enjoyed it, once I had mastered the various declensions, conjugations, case-endings and other niceties which made Latin grammar so much more complicated than French. Mr Stephenson, the headmaster of the primary school, had predicted that I would be good at languages, and he was not far wrong. It was during that summer's holiday at Criccieth that I first became interested in the Welsh language, and picked up a few words and phrases. It was an interest that was set to develop considerably in future years.

There were other changes at the start of the new term. The form-room into which the new III Alpha was to move was too small to accommodate thirty-one boys, and so two had to be drafted temporarily into IIIA which was housed in a larger classroom. I drew the short straw, as did Fred Pakeman. Inevitably, we were seen as interlopers by some, including the class bully and his henchmen who deliberately made life unpleasant, so it was not a happy time, although of course I could still see my old friends in III Alpha at break-times. I consoled myself with the thought that it was only for a year, during which time I would get my head down and try to ignore those who, although they might make things difficult, would count for nothing in the long run. One compensating factor was that our form master was Mr Mitchell, the chemistry teacher who lived on the opposite corner to us. I remember how he entertained us on the last day of the autumn term. Having prepared all kinds of apparatus and experiments during the lunch-time, he put on a display of chemical magic, with liquids and gases that miraculously changed colour, substances that seemed to appear from nowhere, and some spectacular pyrotechnics.

Mr Mitchell retired at the end of my second year, and was replaced by a Mr Thomas, nicknamed 'Alfie'. He was a pleasant enough man who tried to be friendly, but class-control was not his *forte,* and the boys soon cottoned on to it. An anonymously-composed verse began to circulate:

'Down amongst the test-tubes,
The stench begins to rise,
For we are doing Practical,
Under Alfie's eyes.'

He was not, in fact, always as vigilant as he might have been over the handling of dangerous chemicals. One of his demonstrations involved the use of phosphorus, a highly volatile substance, sticks of which had to be stored in water-filled jars so as to prevent the spontaneous combustion that occurs when exposed to the air. 'Alfie' fished a stick of phosphorus out of the jar, and laid it on the laboratory bench while he explained what the experiment was about: not a wise thing to do. He then took a rusty knife out of the drawer and attempted to cut a piece off the stick which by this time had begun to react with the air. Immediately the stick erupted, giving off clouds of fumes and scattering burning fragments across the lab – an incendiary bomb, in fact. Having failed to get the fire-extinguisher down from the wall, 'Alfie' ran out of the lab to get assistance from the upstairs staff-room, leaving us boys to evacuate as best we could. Mr Middlemas, the head of physics, came down and dealt with the situation. Mercifully, no-one was injured.

Another of Alfie's experiments involved the production of coal-gas from crushed-up fragments of coal heated up in a metal pipe with a Bunsen burner. The gas so produced exited through a length of glass tubing and was ignited. We were promised a visit to the town gasworks down by Leek station, but it never materialised. I think he was afraid of what some of us might have got up to in the process, but we kept dropping hints. For example, if he used the word, 'class-work', someone would invariably call out, 'Did you mean gas-works, sir?' He never really regained his confidence after the phosphorus fire, and there is no doubt that some of us boys gave him a hard time. We later learned that after school he would sometimes go off to Ballington Woods on the south side of the town, and pace about for hours to try to calm his shattered nerves.

A favourite port-of-call for many of us boys on the way home from school was the 'Wam Shop' in Wellington Street, where Mrs Keates (no relation of mine as far as I was aware) ran a tiny herbalist shop in a converted front-room, and dispensed home-made herb beer for a penny a half-pint. It was this concoction that we called 'Wam'. It was dispensed from corked bottles, the corks being tied on with string, and they would go 'pop' when opened. 'Wam' was something of an acquired taste, herby as one would expect, and quite bitter. The fizz would have been caused by some kind of fermentation in the bottle; as to any alcoholic content, one can only speculate.

Christmas 1955 set a pattern which was to be followed for many years to come. Since my infant days it had been usual for Auntie Mary and Uncle John, and my four aunts from Northcliff, to come to our house on Christmas Eve to do the 'Santa Thing', and they would stay and have supper after I had been put to bed. Christmas Day was always spent at home, and we would visit various family members on Boxing Day. Until her death in 1954 'Auntie-Auntie' had always gone to Northcliff for Christmas Day. Now, in 1955, it was suggested that my parents and I, and Auntie Mary and Uncle John, would go to Northcliff for Christmas dinner, and that we would all spend Boxing Day together at Lowther Place. So our family Christmas came to be spread over three days; and I remember what jolly times we had, each day being different, but equally enjoyable. The day at Northcliff was punctuated by the production of 'Christmas boxes'. Each of my aunts would bring out a box containing small gifts for everybody, and these were handed out in addition to our main presents which we had received earlier in the day. Mine generally consisted of sweets or chocolates, and pens and other writing and drawing materials which came in very useful,

In the dining room at Northcliff there was a set of handsome Victorian balloon-back chairs. One of my boyish tricks was to wriggle head-first through the hole in the chair-back. One Christmas Auntie Nellie decided to join in the fun and so put her head through the hole and attempted to wriggle through, but she got stuck half way, and was unable to free herself. With help, she managed to stand up, with all four legs of the chair now sticking out in front of her, but she was still firmly held around the midriff. In spite of her predicament, she could see the funny side of the situation, as did some of the others, with the exception of Auntie Mary who went hysterical. 'Chop the chair up! Chop the chair up!' she screamed at the top of her voice, frantically waving her arms in the air. Dad and Uncle John came to the rescue and were able to free Auntie Nellie, while Aunt Mary was consoled with a large whisky. Needless to say, the trick was never repeated.

In 1956 I became head chorister at St Edward's. Those days in the choir had several long-lasting effects. The choir was affiliated to the Royal School of Church Music, and there were regular practices and voice-training sessions. It was at this time of my life that, through regular singing, I came to know by heart so many of the Psalms which have since become a part of my priestly discipline of saying Morning and Evening Prayer. It was also in 1956 that I was confirmed by the Bishop of Stafford, Dr Hammond, whom I remember as a little man with round-framed spectacles and white wavy hair. On the following Sunday I made my first Communion, accompanied by my mother. Holy Communion was celebrated at the early hour of 8 a.m. The service was simply said, without any hymns or other music. Silence reigned as the congregation took their places, then, just before the church clock struck the hour, the vicar and assistant clergy emerged from the sacristy, entered the sanctuary and stood silently in front of the altar. On the final stroke of eight o' clock, the vicar extended his arms and began the 'Our Father' in a subdued voice. There was little of the ceremonial to which I was later attracted, but there was certainly a sense of occasion about it, an atmosphere of deep reverence, and a feeling that here was something very special.

The school curriculum did, of course, include 'R.I.' – Religious Instruction as it was then called, later to be renamed R.E. – Religious Education. Under the terms of what was then known as The Agreed Syllabus, such instruction was to be non-denominational, and mainly Bible-based. At Leek High School there was no specially-trained R.E. teacher. It was commonly believed that any teacher who felt so inclined could handle R.E., and there were some who were drafted into it willy-nilly. To begin with at LHS we were taught by the classics master 'Tut' Gilham, who seemed to have some commitment to the subject. Homework would sometimes consist of learning one or other of the Psalms, and we would be tested the following week. For me, this was no difficult task as I was getting to learn many of the Psalms by heart through singing them in choir. After 'Tut' retired, R.I. lessons were taken by a number of masters who seemed to look on it as a chore, and I have to say that they did little for me.

Among those who had a more profound and lasting influence on my spiritual development were two elderly sisters, Hermione and Stephanie Warren who lived in what had been their parents' home at Southfields, off Southbank Street and in All Saints' parish. Their father had been the first vicar of St Chad's Church at Longsdon, on the road from Leek towards Hanley. There had also been a brother, Hugh. He had followed in his father's footsteps, entered the priesthood, and spent some years overseas as a mission priest before returning to England in the 1950s to become vicar of Cauldon in the Staffordshire moorlands. He died, relatively young, at Christmas in 1956. My first encounter with the Warren family was when the combined choirs of St Edward's and All Saints' sang at his funeral service at Longsdon. Their situation reminded me very much of the Gospel story of Mary, Martha and Lazarus in their home at Bethany: Mary who sat at the Lord's feet, her sister Martha who did all the chores, and the beloved brother Lazarus who died young. Hermione was very much the 'Mary' figure; a devout lady who wrote poetry too, some of which appeared from time to time in the local weekly, the *Leek Post & Times.* She also wrote an article about the Holy Shroud of Turin, allegedly the burial-cloth in which the body of Jesus has been laid to rest after the crucifixion. The article concluded with an invitation to anyone who wished to know more to contact her. It was in response to this that I first visited no. 3 Southfields, a large late-Victorian terraced house overlooking Ladydale. It was a step back in time, rather like Pip – the central character in Dickens' *Great Expectations* – visiting Miss Havisham's time-capsule of a house, except that the Misses Warrens' house was neat and tidy, if somewhat cluttered with Victorian and Edwardian furniture and ornaments. In the front room there was a grand piano, on which stood a number of old family photographs in silver frames. There was a large open fireplace with a big overmantel complete with gas-brackets and glass shades. As late as the 1950s gas-lighting was still in use throughout the house, and electricity was confined to the kitchen.

One of the bedrooms was used as a domestic chapel, with an altar and elaborate furnishings which had been consecrated by a visiting colonial bishop in Father Warren's time. It was here that Hermione sat 'at the Lord's feet', as it were; but although she rarely left the house she was very knowledgeable about world affairs, and of course, those of the Church. She cared passionately about Christian unity, and especially the reunion of the Church of England with the Church of Rome. Like her sister Stephanie, and their parents before them, she was an ardent Anglo-Catholic. It was through Hermione Warren that I learned something of the Church's healing ministry, an interest which has remained with me over the years, like the Turin Shroud which was the cause of my first contact with her. It was Hermione's dearest wish that the house should be known in perpetuity by the name she had given it – The House of St Michael and Our Lady of the Angels – and become a centre for the study and practice of spiritual healing within the Anglican Catholic tradition. Sadly, that wish, along with other arrangements which she had put in place, were set aside following her death in 1994, and the house now functions as a retreat under the name of St Chad's House, which carries at least an echo of the sisters' upbringing at Longsdon vicarage.

In 1956 I acquired my one and only bicycle, for which I had saved up pocket money over a long period of time. I had always been encouraged to be thrifty, and I still have the small cash-box which Auntie Myra bought in Leek Market for just under two shillings (ten pence in modern currency) and in which I put away instalments of pocket money in order to buy the bike. Road traffic was considerably less voluminous and less dangerous in the 1950s, so it was possible to be quite adventurous. I went on several cycling expeditions, either with Cameron Watson, whom I still saw at weekends and during school holidays, or Arthur Massey. The most memorable of these was when we decided to see just how far we could go from Leek in a day. We set off along the Macclesfield Road, cycled through Congleton, Middlewich and Winsford, and as far as the edge of Delamere Forest, about ten miles from Chester; a round trip of about eighty miles! I loved nothing better than going out on my bike into the countryside, either with friends or alone. The rugged uplands around the Roaches, Ramshaw Rocks and Morridge were close by, and also the leafy lanes around Meerbrook, Rushton, and Rudyard Lake.

Ready-made entertainment was still scarce. There were however three cinemas in Leek: the Palace which was not very palatial, the Majestic which was anything but, and the Grand which just about lived up to its name! Memorable films of that era included *The Dam Busters*, and *Forbidden Planet* which I believe to be one of the best science-fiction films ever made because of its stunning special effects and surrealist atmosphere of the planet Altair, all very remarkable for the mid-1950s. There was a little live theatre by way of the plays put on by local amateur dramatic societies, while two local operatic societies put on annual offerings of Gilbert and Sullivan, Léhar, and other light operatic works. Then there was the good old 'steam radio' with favourite programmes like *Take it From Here,* the schools quiz programme *Top of the Form,* and of course *The Goon Show* which I still think is one of the funniest comedy series ever made. There were also comics such as the *Dandy* and the *Beano* to offer light relief from the more serious reading we had to do. I developed a particular liking for Peter Sellers, one of the 'Goons' who was beginning to appear in films such as *I'm Alright, Jack.* He had an immense talent for mimicry, and could put on a vast range of voices and accents which I tried to imitate, to the amusement of some, and the irritation of others. He brought out an LP entitled, *Songs for Swinging Sellers,* and which included a spoof travelogue entitled, 'Balham – Gateway to the South', and 'Common Entrance' which was all about a fifth-rate public school, ending with a comic rendering of 'Nymphs and Shepherds' by the school choir in which Sellers did all the voices, and, inevitably, it always evoked memories of our own school choir.

Peter Sellers starred in the comedy film, *The Smallest Show on Earth.* Released in 1957, the film was about a young couple who inherited a run-down dilapidated cinema called The Bijou which had more than a passing resemblance to Leek's so-called Majestic cinema, which was tucked away down a side-street (Union Street, off Stockwell Street), had patently seen better days, and was anything but majestic. It was run by a bald-headed manager called Mr Marriott, and if the projector broke down – as it seemed often to do – the audience was wont to set up a chant: 'Where's the man with the big bald head?' until the programme resumed. It was, apparently, after some such incident in which LHS boys had allegedly been involved, that the headmaster had the whole school lined up in the assembly hall the following morning. Walking up and down the lines, he questioned each boy individually, 'Were you at the Majestic cinema last evening?' I was able to answer, honestly, 'No', and I never discovered the precise nature of the incident, or who was involved in it. A few years later, in 1961, the Majestic went up in flames one night – like the rival establishment to the 'Bijou' in the comedy film – and a story went around the town that it was no accident either.

We had a comedian within the family, Uncle John, who was fond of practical jokes, and who sometimes regaled me with stories of the things he had got up to as a pupil at Queen Elizabeth Grammar School, Mansfield, and later at University College, Nottingham, where he had trained as a pharmacist. On one occasion he had heated up a laboratory water-tap with a Bunsen burner, and then complained to the chemistry master – who was always boasting about his strength – that he couldn't turn it on. The chemistry teacher burned his hand, and Uncle John got the seat of his pants warmed. His other student escapades had involved putting itching-powder on the seats in a ladies' toilet, and cutting down a tree in Sherwood Forest in order to make a radio mast. Auntie Myra told me that on an early visit to Northcliff, while courting Auntie Mary, he had spotted a pile of Staffordshire oatcakes on the kitchen table, and, never having seen this local delicacy before, was curious to know what they were. Large, round and flat, and soft like a chapatti, they are very different from the Scottish variety, and at this time were virtually unknown outside north Staffordshire. Picking one up, Uncle John is reputed to have said, 'It's just like a ruddy washleather,' before proceeding to wipe it across the wall-mirror. Houseproud Auntie Myra was not amused, but she and her sisters had to get used to his quirky sense of humour. I nicknamed him 'Nunky' after a somewhat shady shopkeeper in the BBC comedy series, *The Navy Lark.* He sometimes said that he should have been locked up for some of the things he had got up to in his younger days.

While at the West Street shop in Leek he concocted an explosive powder which he scattered in the road just before a band of cadets came marching by. Of course they picked it up on their boots and struck sparks from the road surface. On family outings in the car he was always game for a laugh and rarely missed an opportunity to 'perform'. On a coach-trip with the Leek Chamber of Trade over the Horseshoe Pass near Llangollen, he ran after an unwary sheep, captured it, and to the amusement of the bystanders got it to pose – somewhat unwillingly – for a photograph **[27]**. Occasionally Uncle John got paid back in his own kind. My father – who was not entirely devoid of a sense of humour – once hung a tattered old umbrella on a tree not far from the Asher residence, and attached to it a label which read, 'Please return to J.T. Asher, 38, Lowther Place. Finder will be rewarded'.

The photograph of the 'sheep-rustling' incident reveals something else about life in the 1950s that is so different from life today. Even on a day-trip, people tended to dress up rather than dress down. 'Nunky' is wearing a suit and tie, while the ladies are dressed in smart hats and coats.

'Nunky' did of course have his serious side, as befitted a pharmaceutical chemist with his own shop. Well-educated and well-read, he was a mine of information on many subjects. I would often call in at the West Street shop on my way home from school, and in between serving customers we would have many a long chat, about chemistry, history and current affairs, sometimes interspersed with memories of his own schooldays.

They were the kind of conversations that – for a variety of reasons – rarely took place at home. At the back of the shop was the small dispensary where I was introduced to the mysteries of deciphering doctors' prescriptions which were still written in medical Latin, and of mixing medicines from basic ingredients which were kept in blue-glass bottles. These were the days when pharmacists still made up their own mixtures in addition to the proprietary brands sourced from pharmaceutical suppliers, and Uncle John also knew how to make and cut pills, gilding them by putting them into a lidded wooden vessel similar in shape to a shaving-bowl, along with a square of gold leaf, and then shaking it for several minutes, after which the pills would come out evenly coated; quite literally 'gilding the pill'.

One of Uncle John's hobbies was coin-collecting, and most of his collection was housed in a special coin cabinet which he kept in the dispensary. I was allowed to examine the coins, and so became familiar with English coinage going back to the thirteenth century, the oldest coin in the collection being a silver penny dating from King John's reign. 'Nunky' encouraged me to begin my own collection, and I continued to build it up in the years to come.

There were those who said that Uncle John needed a sense of humour in order to live with Auntie Mary, who was somewhat quick-tempered, sharp-tongued, and very different in many other respects too from her sisters. She could also be good fun when the mood suited her, and it was the unpredictability that was difficult to cope with. She was quite happy to bask in the sunshine of Uncle John's successful career as a pharmacist, and to enjoy all the social engagements which stemmed from it; the new dresses, the parties, dinners and balls. On the other hand, poor Uncle John had often to bear the full brunt of her awkwardness and fault-finding, and she was not averse, on occasion, to putting him down in front of other people. I sometimes wonder whether keeping the shop open until 7 p.m. on most weekdays was a matter of choice as well as a matter of necessity. It was in quiet moments at the shop that he copied up the detailed war-time diaries and added the illustrations, because for some odd reason Auntie Mary objected to his working on them at home. She had little to complain about. They were not exactly short of money, there was a succession of new cars, and apart from all the social functions, they were able to get out and about on Thursday afternoons when the shop was shut for half-day closing, and on Sundays too. Sometimes they would call and pick up Mother, Dad and me for a day or a half day's outing in the car, which were spoiled only by an occasional tantrum (or, as Dad called them, 'a touch of the Pollies'), or by the yapping of their poodle, Chérie, which was as highly-strung as its owner, and liable to snap at anyone who went near it. 'Highly strung – and so it should be,' Dad said on more than one occasion. The dog had a weak bladder, or so it seemed given the number of times Uncle John was obliged to stop the car so that it could be taken out to 'tinny' – to use a Nottinghamshire expression. 'Need to squeeze the dog again?' Dad would sometimes ask. Though he generally loved dogs, he had no time whatever for that bundle of yapping nerves which he said was a cross between a sheep and a rat, snapping and snarling at anyone who went near it, apart, that is, from 'Mummy' and 'Daddy'. On such occasions, and also when we went to Northcliff and Lowther Place at Christmas-time, our own little dog Nell had to stay behind at home, for fear of what might happen if the two animals came face-to-face. Chérie could never be parted from her 'Mummy', and she was indeed a child-substitute.

Unpredictable and sometimes cantankerous as Auntie Mary could be, she had her humorous side too, and could be good company. I remember that on a family visit to Llandudno one of my other aunts speculated why it was that one rarely saw cats at the seaside. 'That's because they're all in pies!' Auntie Mary exclaimed, with a chuckle. It tickled my imagination, and I later added witticisms of my own, such as, 'steak and kitty pie… with puss pastry.'

Steak-and-kidney pudding, with suet pastry, was undoubtedly my favourite dish at home, and it was routinely served up every Thursday, when I would come home from school to find the pudding-basin, neatly capped and tied, boiling away in a big saucepan on the stove. Thursday was firmly my favourite weekday, partly because the weekend was now in sight, because it was sometimes train-spotting day at Leek station, but above all else because it was steak-and-kidney pudding day. Though never overweight, I had a very robust appetite, and Auntie Mary said more than once that she would rather keep me for a week than a fortnight.

My father had never enjoyed the best of health. Winter almost always saw him go down with some chest problem, and he had an almost permanent cough, exacerbated no doubt by smoking cigarettes; but then most men smoked in those days, and few were then aware of the serious health hazards it could cause. One day in 1956 he was late home from work, very late, and my mother became very anxious. Then an ambulance arrived, and it was obvious that something awful had happened. Dad had stayed on at work that evening to finish off a job. A fuse had blown, cutting off the power to his machine, but instead of calling an electrician to investigate, he got a ladder and climbed up himself to the fuse-box. He slipped and fell, and was quite badly injured. Consequently he was off work for over three months, and there was some doubt as to whether he would be capable of going back to his old job. There were some further complications. Because Dad had been injured while, in effect, doing an electrician's job for which he was not qualified, there was doubt as to whether he would be entitled to any compensation, and an industrial tribunal eventually ruled against him. All of this had serious financial consequences for us. Great-aunt Myra's legacy, which might otherwise have been used to help buy our own home, was drawn upon to pay weekly bills, and my father's pride would not allow him to take advantage of offers of help from my aunts. He would not let my mother go out to work; he believed it was his responsibility to support us. At the same time he insisted that household management – paying bills, managing the housekeeping money, shopping, cooking and cleaning – were the wife's responsibility, and he would have no part in them.

At this time, Dad became progressively alienated from his brothers. It had – so I was told – partly to do with the settlement of his father's affairs, and also the care of my grandmother who had lately had a bad fall and fractured her femur. She remained an invalid for the rest of her life. There appear to have been other disputes amongst the brothers, the details of which I never fully knew or understood, but one consequence was – tragically – that it rubbed off on the younger generation. It was a very difficult time, and although things were eventually patched up between Dad and his brother Dennis, he remained at odds with the other two brothers to the end of his life. He refused to attend the family gathering after his mother's funeral in 1965, and he also made it clear that – should anything happen to him – they should not be invited to his. I was later to have the awful duty of complying with this request. To this day, I profoundly regret the enforced alienation from my father's side of the family, and its legacy of bitterness and damaged friendships. How painfully true was that Old Testament proverb, 'The fathers have eaten a sour grape, and the children's teeth are set on edge' (*Jeremiah* 31.29).

The accident, the consequent financial worries, and the problems within his family, help to explain why Dad seemed to become very bad-tempered and difficult to get on with at this time. It was virtually a character-change. Though extremely patient in some ways – especially when setting his mind to some piece of engineering, or sitting fishing by the canal – he had always had a stern and sombre side to him, and was given to silent brooding and occasional outbursts of extreme anger. We saw and heard much more of this from the time of the accident onwards, and there were some quite ugly scenes which I found extremely frightening, though I have to say that he was never physically violent towards me or my mother. It was, however, like walking on eggshells. The slightest thing could trigger an outburst, and sometimes I found it easier to keep my mouth shut and my head down. He seemed to disapprove of my school-friends, the subjects I most enjoyed at school – such as history and French which he thought were a waste of time – and most of the things I was interested in. Local and national institutions, such as the Crown, the Church, national and local government, all came under attack. Consequently I became increasingly withdrawn and quiet, very guarded in what I said, and spending a lot of time out of the house whenever I could. Northcliff became ever more a place of refuge where I could share my thoughts and have meaningful conversations about anything and everything, and there were times when I heartily wished I could have moved in there. All of this was very sad, and I do not entirely blame my father, for with hindsight I can understand the pressures and stresses he was under at this time. Things were probably never quite as bad as they seemed, and the situation gradually improved as I got older; but those were the adolescent years when things are taken very much to heart, when I ought really to have been much closer to my father and enjoyed his company and confidence. Instead I felt frightened, alienated, very insecure, and was even ill for a time. The doctor said that I looked 'harassed', which was a fair diagnosis of my condition, but that did nothing to improve Dad's health and temper.

Although Dad enjoyed a pint or two of beer, he never drank during the week, but generally just on Saturday evening when he would meet friends in one of their customary 'watering holes'. He never drank to excess, but a couple of pints of beer would sometimes loosen his tongue, and make him more than usually argumentative and bad-tempered. I would therefore usually make sure that I had gone to bed before he returned home, although even then I could sometimes hear a raised voice coming from the living room as he fired off about one issue or another. 'Beer talking again', mother would sometimes say, and she shrugged it off much better than I ever could.

There were some long-term consequences to all of this. The habit of withdrawing into my 'shell' when feeling threatened has never entirely gone away; nor can I bear anyone to pry, to snoop, to look over my shoulder, or otherwise invade my personal space. My intense dislike of swearing and violent language goes back to those days when my young ears heard a fair bit of it, although the 'bloodies' and the 'buggers' were mild in comparison to what is considered acceptable in some circles nowadays. Nevertheless it upset my mother, and I vowed then that no-one would ever hear me use language like that. I still firmly believe that so-called 'strong language' lends neither force to the argument nor dignity to the speaker.

Gradually, I built a kind of defensive wall around myself, which grew ever higher, and which in the end became a prison from which I found difficulty in escaping, and it most certainly inhibited the forming of meaningful relationships. How I wished then, and for some time to come, that I had a 'soul mate' of my own age with whom I could be completely open and honest, share my deepest thoughts and feelings, without running the risk of being ridiculed or shot down in flames. That feeling of insecurity inevitably had an effect on my school-life. I was easily intimidated – something which one or two of the 'bully-boys' cottoned on to – and some of the masters appeared so overbearing that I was afraid to speak out or to ask questions when I was in difficulty, especially in maths lessons.

During my third year at LHS – 1956-7 – the time came to decide my 'O' level options. Weakness in maths meant that I

[1] Derby Street, Leek, looking towards 'The Monument'.
In the foreground is the Roebuck Inn, next to which is Tatton's Café.
The History and Heritage of Leek & the Staffordshire Moorlands.

[2] View over the north of the town, with the Nicholson Institute far right;
the town hall and the Brunswick chapel (now demolished)
and the parish church tower beyond.
The History and Heritage of Leek & the Staffordshire Moorlands.

[3] Leek Market Place with the old market cross reinstated. Photo - Neil Collingwood.

[4] My parents about to go on honeymoon, September 1941.

[5] Ellen Carding, second from left, and her sisters Sarah, Lizzie, Myra and Susan, c. 1890.

[6] Clifford Keates in Royal Artillery uniform, c. 1890.

[7] St Edward's church bells prior to re-hanging, 1907.

[8] Writing box made by Clifford Keates from 'belfry oak'.

[9] Grandmother Ellen Keates and her family, c.1930.

Back row –
Dorothy, Ellen, Lizzie.

Front row –
Nellie, Flossie, Mary, Myra.

[10] Uncle John Asher. MPS, c. 1955.

[11] The Corner Pharmacy, West Street, Leek.

[12] St Edward's Church viewd from the top of Mill Street.
Photo – Basil Turner courtesy of Barry & Gwen Turner.

[13] MF aged two, on the rocking swan made by his father.

[14] A sole survivor from childhood days – the brass and copper steam engine.

[15] Westwood Road School group. MF on front row, far left.

[16] On holiday at Abergele, 1947. Dad said that Mum looked like 'the Belsen kommandant'!

[17] One of Dad's sand sculptures, on the beach at Lytham St Annes.

[18] Dieulacres Abbey ruins, with the lower slopes of Hillswood beyond.

[19] Leek Cattle Market on the former Haywood Street site.
The History and Heritage of Leek & the Staffordshire Moorlands.

[20] Leek Railway Station c. 1960
looking towards the town gasworks.
Robert Tatton

[21] Club Day procession in July.
The History and Heritage of Leek & the Staffordshire Moorlands.

[22] Nellie and Dorothy Keates behind the counter
at the Stanley Street Wool Shop.

[23] St Edward's church choir c. 1953. MF standing on second row just in front of the cross. Nearby is organist Ada Parr, the curate (the Revd. Hubbard) and George Youell, vicar.
Robed choirboys on front row: Geoffrey Staton, Barry Whittaker, Stuart Shingler, -?-, Barry Hollinshead, Phillip Mitchell, Stephen Wibberley, Anthony Shatwell, Anthony Fowler.

[24] Outside the Octagon at Alton Towers, c.1951.

[25] The wool shop, Stanley Street. Coronation window 1953.

[26] In Leek High School uniform, with friend Cameron Watson, 1954.

[27] The sheep rustler –
'Nunky' up to one of his antics.

[28] Leek High School 1960. Third row, seated – C.K.R. Pearce (headmaster), Messrs Goodwin, Chapman, Burton, Roberts, Lazarus, 'Mademoiselle', D.N. Jones, N. Thomas, T.R. Jones, Conway.

[29] On stage in 'Housemaster' as Button Farington, with my stage brother, Tony Fowler.

[30] Start of Leek High School visit to Austria, 1960, with staff member D.N. ('Dizzy') Jones.

Leek Post & Times

[31] September 1961 – Silver wedding celebrations at Southbank Hotel. MF, Auntie Myra and her cousin Flossie Johnson, and great-aunt Sarah, then our oldest living relative.
Leek Post & Times

[32] 1950s ladies fashions Aunts Mary, Nellie, Myra, Dorothy and Flossie.

could not easily specialise in sciences. This was a disappointment. I enjoyed chemistry, and was quite good at it, but physics was far less strong, no doubt because of its high mathematical content. So I went on to the arts side – French, Latin, geography, history and English literature, along with English language and maths which everybody took. I was sorry to have to give up art and handicraft; these subjects were continued only by those who dropped foreign languages at this stage. I had a fondness for drawing and calligraphy both of which I was able to pursue in my spare time; and a lot that I learned from 'Dizzy' Jones in the woodwork room has proved useful in later life, so I am grateful for what he taught us about timber and wood-joints. This complemented what I learned from my father through observation and helping with odd jobs around the house, painting and wallpapering. Amongst other things, Dad showed me how to paper a ceiling single-handed. These inherited practical skills, and his insistence on accuracy in all things, have helped to counterbalance memories of the negative side of our relationship which was a part of my growing up.

During my 'O' level years there were some significant staff changes. 'Tut' Gilham, the classics master, retired, and was replaced by Mr Glenny, a somewhat portly gentleman whose rotund abdomen earned him the nickname 'Pot', because he was 'always out at the front' and was also known as 'Uncle Stan' amongst the classics scholars. In 1957 old Mr Walmesley, the history teacher, retired too, and I was sorry to see the departure of this fine and kindly teacher who had done a great deal to encourage me. Everyone had a high regard for 'Wigwam' and many of us kept in touch with him after his retirement when he continued to live a bachelor life in his house in Westwood Road. Regrettably, his farewell on the last day of the summer term was marred by a riot which broke out on the school field, and its dire consequences. Following some incident in the playground at morning break, the duty master had cleared the area and sent all the boys involved out on to the sports field facing Westwood Road. At the end of break, around fifty of them refused to come back into school, and sat in protest on the wall which separated the field from the Westwood Recreation Ground. Eventually they were rounded up and brought back inside. The headmaster took control, and, acting like a sergeant-major, he made all the offenders stand in straight lines in the inner quadrangle, and there they were forced to remain, in the stand-at-ease position, for the rest of the morning and into the afternoon. It was a hot sunny day, and one or two of them collapsed in the heat.

Mr Walmesley was replaced by the young Mr David Conway, who soon earned the nickname 'Flicker' because of a habit of flicking back his hair. There was a change at the top too. Mr Ramsay, whose sight had been failing for some time, finally became completely blind, so he took early retirement, and was replaced as headmaster by Mr Charles Pearce, who had been Head of English at King Edward VI Grammar School, Stafford. When, in 1967, I joined the staff of that school, I instantly recognised the source of several of the innovations which Mr Pearce had introduced to LHS, such as house assemblies, and a distinctive uniform for sixth-formers. The uniform rule had become somewhat lax during Mr Ramsay's last years, and although the maroon blazer, grey flannels and school tie were still *de rigueur* in the lower school, fifth formers were allowed to wear sports jackets and a tie of a specified range of colours. Mr Pearce now insisted on the appropriate uniform for all. On the other hand, he did away with some of the relics of the previous régime such as the military-style dismissal-drill at the end of morning assembly, and the permanent numbers.

I was at this time beginning to develop my religious ideas and inclinations, which tended ever more towards Anglo-Catholicism. Two of my aunts had been greatly influenced in their teenage years by the Revd Jasper Stoneman Caiger, who was vicar of St Edward's just after the First World War. He had helped my grandmother to come to terms with my grandfather's death in 1917, and she had held him in high regard. He was a product of St Stephen's House, Oxford, and therefore strongly Anglo-Catholic. His time at St Edward's was cut short by those who disapproved of his brand of churchmanship and of the innovations he brought with him, and they petitioned for his removal. His influence, however, remained with those who had approved of him, and I believe that some of my earliest Catholic sympathies stemmed ultimately from that source, and from the devotional books which were still around at Northcliff. I still have a little illustrated booklet given to me by Auntie Flossie when I was about five years old. It has pictures of the Mass, and an exposition of the Mass for young children, and quite clearly is of Roman-Catholic origin. Then there were those memorable visits to the Catholic sites at Alton to which I have already referred. When living at Sneyd Avenue we were close enough to St Mary's Catholic Church to hear the Angelus rung at the appropriate hour, and I came to know what it signified. I once ventured inside to St Mary's to see what it was like, as I had been led to believe that Catholics were of a different race – if not of a different planet! To my surprise, I discovered that its furnishings were not so very different from the ones to which I was accustomed at St Edward's – altar, pulpit, lectern, pews, stained-glass windows – if somewhat more elaborate. Nuns from the King Street convent were a familiar sight on the streets of the town, usually in pairs, and in the full flowing black-and-white habit of pre-Vatican II days. I remember too visiting my grandparents in Frith Street not long after they had acquired a television set. They were watching what was in those days a very rare thing – a live broadcast from continental Europe. It was a High Mass broadcast from the cathedral of Notre Dame in Paris. I can remember watching the celebrant censing the altar, and the drama of the Latin Mass unfolding before me, and I was fascinated by it. My mother once told me that Grandma Fisher and her younger sister, Harriet, had been born into a Catholic family, and had lapsed only at the time of their respective marriages. From the Leek Public Library I later borrowed a book entitled *Our Faith*, only to discover that it was in fact a Roman Catholic book written by a future Archbishop of Westminster, John Carmel Heenan, but it all seemed to make sense to me, especially what was written about the central focus of Catholic life, the Mass.

St Edward's Parish Church was what in those days would have been described as middle-of-the-road Anglican, with Mattins and Evensong as the main Sunday services. Father Caiger had tried to introduce the Sung Eucharist as the principal morning service, but after his departure it had been relegated once again to the early hour, and was said rather than sung. The vicar of St Edward's from 1952 was archdeacon George Youell, also a St Stephen's House man, and with Catholic sympathies, but he moved slowly and eventually managed to achieve a monthly Choral Eucharist, but at 8 a.m. and with a volunteer choir. To the 'old guard' Mattins at 10.30 was sacrosanct. Eventually my voice began to break, and I was no longer able to sing in the choir. I had been trained as a server, but for fear of upsetting the protestant 'old guard', servers were not used on Sundays, only at the early-morning weekday celebrations when the 'opposition' was not likely to be present anyway. So I took my turn at 7 a.m. Knowing that I had gone out of the house very early one morning, my father asked my mother where I had gone, and when she told him he 'played hallelujah', as the saying went.

To my eager mind, it was in any case too slow, and my attention was drawn to All Saints' Church on the south side of the town, which was known to be 'High', with a Sung Eucharist at 9 a.m. on Sundays. So I began to attend All Saints', to the disappointment no doubt of archdeacon Youell, and most certainly to the disappointment of my mother and her sisters who had strong family attachments to St Edward's. There was another motive too. All Saints' was the church which my father and his brothers had attended in their younger days, until they all left in a huff following an argument with the vicar about the club-room they had helped to build at the east end of the church. Dad had never set foot inside All Saints' since then, and he said on more than one occasion that he did not wish to be taken there in his coffin either. However, I naively imagined – and even prayed – that my going there might one day draw him back into the fold. I rather think it had the reverse effect. On one occasion when Dad was ill in bed I mentioned the fact to the parish priest, Fr. Norman Turner. Out of kindness and concern, he paid a visit, but Dad flatly refused to allow him into the bedroom. There was some shouting, and poor Fr. Turner left rather abruptly, and to my mother's acute embarrassment, and mine too. Thus, contrary to what I had hoped, the church became yet another obstacle in the already shaky relationship between father and son.

I learned to be extremely cautious over the use of religious pictures and devotional aids, following a particularly unpleasant incident which still haunts me from time to time. I had mounted some small pictures – one of which was of the Crucifixion – on some gold-coloured card, in the form of a triptych, slightly reminiscent of the altarpiece at All Saints', and pinned it up in my bedroom. Not long afterwards Dad discovered it, and went 'ballistic'. Mother was summoned, and I was ordered out of the bedroom while they undertook a thorough search for any similar items. As I sat in the living room I could hear the sound of drawers and cupboards being opened and closed as they were systematically ransacked. I doubt if the discovery of pornographic magazines under my bed and 'girlie' pictures on the wall would have produced a more angry reaction! Though I came to realise that my father was projecting on to me his own hang ups and long standing resentments about the Church in general and All Saints' Church in particular, as it then stood this invasion of my personal space, to say nothing of the assault on my religious sensibilities, only served to reinforce my feelings of insecurity and isolation.

This was by no means the only time that religious concerns got me into hot water. In my class at school there was a solitary Roman Catholic boy named John. For some reason his parents had decided to send him to Leek High School rather than to one of the Catholic schools such as Cotton College. In those pre-ecumenical days it was the custom for Roman Catholic children in etate schools to be exempted from morning assembly and from the weekly religious education lessons. When it came to R.E., John would sit to one side of the class and occupy himself with some suitable reading, usually the Douay Bible which was the Catholic alternative to the Authorised Version. Consequently he found himself victimised and subjected to some very cruel and nasty verbal abuse on account of his faith. I thought this was dreadful, and more than once I intervened to try to stop it. The inevitable result was that I was also set upon and accused of being a secret Catholic by the bully-boys who prided themselves on their 'protestantism', although I am sure that they had not the slightest idea of what a protestant really was. It was sheer bigotry, doubtless inherited from equally ignorant and prejudiced parents, and I am sorry to say that similar attitudes persist in some quarters even today.

Some of these prejudices seemed to have been reinforced by the way in which the history of the sixteenth and seventeenth centuries was taught in schools, and by the slanted content of some history books. Thus, much emphasis was laid on the negative side of Mary Tudor ('Bloody Mary') and the persecution of protestants during the five years of her reign, but comparatively little was said about the murderous persecution of Catholics that ensued under Elizabeth I and continued until the end of the following century, or the exclusion of Catholics from public life that persisted until the 1820s, or the monstrous ill-treatment of

Catholic Ireland at the hands of successive British governments and protestant landlords.

Then there was the legalised vandalism that accompanied the Reformation: the pillage of the monasteries – including our local Dieulacres Abbey in which I had more than a passing interest – and later the destruction of thousand years' accumulation of religious art and craft in the cathedrals and parish churches, to say nothing of the contents of monastic libraries. I came to wonder if the Reformation had brought any benefits at all. I think it was John Henry Newman who said that to be deep in history was to cease to be protestant; it is most certainly a fair assessment of the opinions that I came to hold. I heartily wished that the Pilgrimage of Grace had succeeded in halting the dissolution of the monasteries, and that the sacrilegious tyrant Henry VIII had been brought to book. My heroes of the period were not Thomas Cranmer, Francis Drake or Walter Raleigh, but Sir Thomas More and Bishop John Fisher. I concluded that Protestantism was a wholly negative force to which I thought I owed very little, except perhaps the so-called 'work ethic' and a duty to develop and use whatever talents I had been given. Later I came to hold a much more balanced view, but those were heady teenage years in which most things were viewed in black and white.

My political opinions were also beginning to take shape at that time. My father was somewhat left-of-centre, although the failure of his union (the Amalgamated Engineering Union) to secure compensation following his accident had disillusioned him about the effectiveness of trade unions. The only politician he openly expressed admiration for, apart from Churchill as a wartime leader, was Clement Davies, a Liberal who had served in Lloyd George's governments. My mother, like her sisters, was cast in the Conservative mould, and it was from them that I took my political inclinations. I can remember sitting in the kitchen at Northcliff at the time of the 1955 election listening to the results coming in over the radio. All the constituencies and their candidates were listed in one of the national papers, with spaces to fill in the results, and I can remember writing these in as they were announced. I joined the Young Conservatives, and got involved in the next election campaign which was the one of 1959. Socialism was, to my mind, not far removed from communism, and the atheistical régimes of central and Eastern Europe, where the Church was persecuted, and where the pro-liberal uprsisings of 1956 were put down with brute force by Russian tanks.

The Leek constituency was at that time held by Labour, and the sitting candidate was Harold Davies, a Welshman from the valleys who had won the seat in the Labour landslide of 1945. Labour had been ousted from power in 1951, and the Conservatives increased their majority in 1955, but Labour managed to hold on to Leek. Harold Davies was a rather likeable man, and most certainly a good constituency M.P. He therefore attracted a personal following including many, I dare say, who were not really Labour supporters at heart, but who voted for the man rather than for the party. Local council elections showed that the town of Leek, and the surrounding villages, were far from being Labour heart-land. The big Labour vote came from places such as Biddulph, Kidsgrove and Brown Edge, areas adjacent to Stoke-on-Trent, yet which had somehow been attached to the Leek constuituency. Though Harold Davies had not a large majority, he had a power-base that would take some shifting. He was a knowledgeable and much-travelled man, and I later invited him to the school to talk to the Geographical Society about a recent visit to Cambodia, which in those days was not an easy place for Westerners to access. His talk was illustrated with movie film he had taken out there, including his exploration of the ancient temples of Angkor Wat, the largest complex of religious buildings in the world.

The candidate adopted by the Leek Conservatives for the 1959 election was Sir John Wedgwood, a descendant of the famous Josiah Wedgwood. It was considered, amongst other things, that his local connections would stand him in good stead. I can remember groups of schoolchildren singing a rhyme, adapted, I think, from a playground skipping song:

> 'Vote, vote, vote for Harold Davies,
> Wedgwood comes knocking at the door,
> Wedgwood is our man,
> And we'll have him if we can,
> But we don't want Harold Davies any more,
> Shut the door.'

The climax of the campaign came with the eve-of-poll meetings. The Labour faithful held their rally at the Palace Cinema, while the Conservatives usually had theirs at the Grand, on the opposite side of the road. As I remember, the ending of these rallies had to be carefully timed, as it was not unknown for the party which finished first to go over the road to heckle and barrack the opposition meeting.

In spite of a further national swing to the Conservatives in 1959, and a big majority for them in the new Parliament, the Leek constituency decided that it *did* still want Harold Davies, and he was to continue as M.P. for Leek until 1970. That was not the last I was to see of the Wedgwood family. Although Sir John did not stand for Leek again, I later came to know his son, Martin, and his daughter-in-law, Alexandra (*née* Alexandra Gordon Clark), who was architectural archivist at the House of Lords, an authority on the work of A.W.N. Pugin.

To coincide with the general election of 1959 it had been decided to hold a mock election at school. It was in part an educational exercise to show how parliamentary democracy worked, and it was to be run as nearly as possible to the real thing, with returning officers, election agents, hustings, election manifestoes, and at the end of it all a secret ballot. I was put forward as the Conservative candidate, and my 'agent' was Alan Machin. We went to the local Conservative Office and had instruction from the constituency agent, Herbert Jones, who taught us how to run a campaign properly. Before becoming an agent, Bert Jones had been a Conservative Trade Unionist in the railway workshops at Crewe, and he had stood unsucessfully as a parliamentary candidate in the Lancashire constituencies of Newton-le-Willows and Bootle. He had a refreshing, down-to-earth approach, hated snobbery, and had a wicked sense of humour. It was people like Bert Jones who showed that it was no strange thing to be both working-class and Conservative, and that it was basically a matter of ideology, not sociology. He armed us with leaflets and posters, showed me how to put together a local manifesto, and taught us about the legal side of elections; what was permissible under the law, and what was not.

The odd thing about the school election was the absence of a Labour candidate. There was a Communist (Pete Richmond), a Liberal (Roderick Barker) and myself as Conservative. In the end, I fared rather better than Sir John Wedgwood, and was elected with quite a big majority. The mock election taught me something else too. In spite of the diffidence, reticence and lack of self-confidence from which I had suffered, when it came to putting up a fight of this kind I was able to rise to the challenge. I had to get up on my feet in front of a crowd and put over a message, to answer questions, and to deal with hecklers. It was a very good exercise in confidence-building, and I rather enjoyed it. Other opportunities came my way. I got involved with the school dramatic society, and took part in two stage productions: Ian Hay's comedy, *Housemaster*, and André Obey's *Noah* in which I had one of the leading roles. Since LHS was an all-male school, and contacts with the girls' high school were – in those days – almost non-existent, female roles were played by boys. My part in *Housemaster* was as the fourteen-year-old tomboy 'Button' Farington. Dresses and a wig were borrowed, and the few photographs I have of the performance still make me shudder with embarrassment, although few at the time saw anything odd in this bit of theatrical licence. The role of my aunt Barbara was played by Garth Turner, another member of St Edward's Church, and a future ordinand and canon of Manchester Cathedral. A fellow chorister, Tony Fowler, was my stage-brother, 'Bimbo' (!) Farington [**29**]. Performing in front of an audience seemed to come to me naturally, whether in the dramatic sense, or public speaking, or giving talks. It was in one-to-one relationships that I was to experience the most difficulty, and where I would often feel awkward. I would also tend to avoid any confrontational situation in which I might find myself under attack, and would prefer to remain silent rather than risk getting hurt. I think this may have been the product of some of those childhood experiences and stormy scenes at home to which I have already referred. Their effect upon me has never entirely gone away.

Chuck Berry is the name of a rock-and-roll singer popular in the 1950s. 'Chuck-berry' was also the name of a game devised by certain members of the lower fifth. The 'berry' was a rugby sock stuffed with newspaper and knotted to form a missile which could be 'chucked' from one side of the classroom to the other when the teacher's back was turned. The object of the game was to see how many times the berry could be thrown between chuckers and catchers in any one lesson without its being spotted by the master.

The School Geographical Society was important to me. I became its secretary, and in this role I had to contact potential speakers and help plan the activities, and a small group of us decided to produce a magazine for the society. We called it *The Globe,* and it contained a wide range of articles submitted by members of the society, such as accounts of visits abroad, or interesting facts about our own area. The editorial team included Alan Machin, Anthony

Brown and Simon Newall. We typed up the material on the staff-room typewriter which was loaned to us for the purpose, and then we ran off the copies on a Gestetner duplicator and stapled it all together. Through the good offices of Bert Jones, the Conservative agent, who had rather better reprographic facilities, we were able to include photographs for which special stencils had to be prepared. All of this gave me valuable experience in the basics of editing and formatting a small in-house magazine and preparing it for publication; skills that I was to develop in later life. I have no doubt that these extra-curricular activities at school also provided an element of stability at times when things could be somewhat difficult at home.

In the year before I sat my 'O' levels we moved from Spring Gardens to a brand-new maisonette in Westwood Heath Road. The lady who owned our house had decided that after all she wanted to return to Leek to be close to her sister, and so my parents had to look for alternatives. Dad's accident had meant, amongst other things, that a home of our own was a much more distant prospect, so we moved once again into rented accommodation, the landlords this time being the local council. It was, however, newly-built, and very pleasantly situated opposite the old sandstone lodge at the bottom of Westwood Park Drive. There was a large garden at the back, which sloped upwards to the boundary of the playing fields of my old junior school, and the high school was only five minutes' walk away, and visible from the living-room window. Mother, however, took a dislike to it and wanted to move again. Amongst other things she missed the former neighbours, Mr and Mrs Moss. She never settled at Westwood, and I remember that my father once said in desperation that if ever she got to heaven she would spend all her time wondering what the 'other place' was like. There was indeed a restless side to my mother's character. I would sometimes come home at lunch-time to find that she had moved all the furniture around in the living-room or one of the bedrooms. When I came home at tea-time it would all have been put back again.

Before we moved to Westwood, Dad made some new kitchen furniture using timber from a very large Victorian/Edwardian wardrobe that had come from great-aunt Myra's house. It had drawers in the bottom, and it reached almost to the ceiling in my bedroom. There would not have been room for it at the flat, and in any case there were built-in wardrobes, so Dad 'recycled' it into more practical items.

Soon after our move to Westwood Heath Road, Nell escaped, met a black labrador dog, and a few weeks later gave birth to a litter of pups. Two of them stayed around for quite some time, and we wondered if we would ever home them. They were delightful; one was all black and the other, like Nell, had white on his paws, chest and muzzle. We named them Blackie and Toby.

The garden, as I have said, was quite a large one, and at this time Dad became very interested in growing speciality dahlias which he tended most carefully. At this time also he moved from Bode's Engineering Works to a new job with Sr T. & A. Wardle along the Macclesfield Road where he worked until his final illness and death in 1970. Wardles were silk manufacturers and dyers. Dad's job as a precision engineer was machine maintenance, and the firm came to depend on him a great deal to keep the wheels moving – literally. Unfortunately the pay did not match up to the responsibilities. He was also working in a hazardous environment, among various toxic chemicals that were used in the textile industry, and there was always a distinctive smell of dyestuffs in the air along that part of Macclesfield Road. I have no doubt that this affected Dad's health in the long term.

Apart from the in-fighting within the Labour Party over nuclear weapons, a major reason for the Conservatives' landslide victory in 1959 was that Labour was associated in many people's minds with post-war austerity, and also with financial mismanagement. The mid-fifties saw a marked upturn in the economy, and most people seemed to benefit from it. After the establishment of the Health Service and the other great social reforms of the late 1940s, Labour now appeared as a party that had run out of steam, and was also divided. On the other hand, the Conservatives were associated (rightly or wrongly) with the 'boom' years of the mid-fifties, and Harold MacMillan, who became prime minister in 1959, coined the phrase, 'You've never had it so good'.

One of the big issues at that time – and for some years to come – was Britain's application to join what was then known as the European Economic Community, i.e. the 'Common Market' as it was then called, which had evolved after the Second World War and which was formally established in 1957 under the Treaty of Rome. There were obvious economic benefits to be had in being part of a single market, and the Conservative government made several attempts to join the 'club' but were vetoed each time by the French president, Charles de Gaulle. Though initially I favoured Britain's membership of the Common Market, I became much less enthusiastic when it morphed into the 'European Union' with all the political consequences such as loss of national sovereignty, and subsequently I became a 'Brexiteer'.

Certainly there was more money in people's pockets by the mid-fifties. There were more consumer goods, such as television sets, radiograms (the precursor of the hi-fi), washing-machines and cars. Young people were now being targeted commercially too, with the advent of teenage fashions. Everybody of a certain age remembers the 'Teddy Boys'. Pop music as we know it began with Bill Hayley and the Comets, and the film *Rock Around the Clock*. Early television programmes devoted to teenage pop included *The Six-five Special,* an early evening Saturday weekly featuring a very young Cliff Richard. *Juke Box Jury* appeared around the same time, also commercial television to break the monopoly of the BBC. Radio still had a powerful hold, with small portable sets now becoming widely available. The *Goon Show* remained a firm favourite with many people, and Goonish expressions such as, 'It's all in the mind, you know', 'He's fallen in the water', 'I don't wish to know that', and 'Niddle-naddle-noo' passed into everyday speech.

Foreign travel was becoming more popular and affordable, and there were opportunities within the school to take advantage of 'school journeys' as they were called. One such was to Belgium in the summer holidays of 1958, and I was fortunate to be able to take part in what at the time seemed a very big adventure: first a train journey to London, an overnight stop, then a ferry from Dover to Ostend. We then travelled by train to Bouillon, in the heart of the Ardennes where we spent a few days exploring the locality before moving on to Brussels. The great attraction was the international exhibition – Expo '58 – which was the first big event of its kind after the war.

England was still at that time a relatively safe place in which to live. Drugs, and violence on the streets, were virtually unknown. It really was possible – in places like Leek at any rate – to go out and leave doors unlocked, and to walk in the towns at night without fear of being attacked. There were dangers, of course, and I was made aware of some of them. I remember as a child being warned to beware of 'funny men', but who these men were, and why they were supposed to be 'funny' remained a mystery until, in the mid-1950s a number of local men were brought before the courts in a series of trials which were widely reported in the local press. The 'funny men' were what we would nowadays describe as paedophiles. A rather pathetic moon-faced young man who kept a gents' outfitters shop in the Market Place was in the habit of chasing young boys down Derby Street, leaving his shop completely unattended. There was a middle-aged projectionist and bingo-caller at one of the Leek cinemas, who had a collection of his own films in a shed at the bottom of his garden, to which he was alleged to entice young boys. Then there was the coal-merchant who delivered to our neighbours in Spring Gardens, and who always seemed to have one or two boys riding on his coal-wagon. All of them were brought to book, and sentenced as they deserved. Neither myself nor any of my immediate friends had ever fallen into the clutches of 'The Boys' as they were collectively known, but while the trials were on we noted who was absent from school on certain days and drew our own conclusions. Very serious though it all was, it also occasioned a certain amount of black comedy within the school, and this ran on for a long time. The words 'shed' and 'bingo' were introduced at every possible juncture. I suspect that the teachers knew very well what we were getting at. We now know, of course, that sexual exploitation of children was more widespread than had been realised at that time, and that it occurred in the most unlikely places.

As I prepared for the 'O' level exams, I had also to give some thought as to what I might do afterwards. Uncle John had rather hoped, quite naturally, that I might take up pharmacy as a career. I did indeed consider it, but I had in the end gone on to the arts side. There was a possibility that I might become an articled clerk with a local solicitor. Dad said that he didn't much mind what I did, so long as I didn't follow him into engineering, or follow up another idea I had toyed with, namely the ordained ministry. There was not very much careers advice available within the school at this time, as I remember

The 'O' level results came out in August 1959. I did reasonably well, but not spectacularly, with five passes out of seven. I had expected to do badly in maths, but to have failed English literature as well came as a surprise and a disappointment because it was a subject I enjoyed, and I thought I knew my set books well. The period during which I studied for 'O levels had been fraught with all kinds of personal upheavals, traumas and emotional upsets, and I have no doubt that these had a detrimental effect on my exams. It was decided nevertheless that I would return to school in September, take history, Latin and French to 'A' level, and re-sit 'O' level maths. Quite a number of my friends left school at this stage to start work or to take up apprenticeships. Martin Knowles, for example, went into his father's butchery business, where there were ready-made opportunities, and he eventually opened a shop of his own. Among the friends who stayed on into the sixth form were Brian Rushton, who was also a server at All Saints', Alan Machin, and Geoff Hampson.

Sixth-form life was somewhat different from that in the lower school. There were privileges and responsibilities; a timetable which included a fair amount of free time which we were expected to use for private study in the library, and there was reading to be done over and above the set books and texts. The classes were of course quite small, and generally run like tutorials with time for discussion and questioning. Solomon Lazarus was my form-master as well as my French teacher, but in the sixth form we saw a different side to one who lower down in the school had appeared stern and somewhat fearsome. He became our guide and mentor. At the end of the two years we even had a collection to buy him a present, and when, some years later, Old Sol retired, a good many old boys took the trouble to attend his farewell.

I was still very much involved with the Geographical Society, and activities were extended to include geological field-trips on Saturdays. Small groups would go off to places such as the Manifold Valley where there were fossils to be found as well as copper and galena on the old spoil-tips by the Ecton mines; or to Cauldon Lowe quarries, or places in the Derbyshire Peak District. James Hollinshead, who was a year or so ahead of me and was taking geology to 'A' level, would often join us, and that was the bginning of a lifelong friendship. Among those from the lower school who joined the society was Mick Rose, who was also a member of All Saints' choir. The next time I encountered Mick, after leaving school, was over thirty years later when I found him working in a hotel in St David's.

In about 1959 Auntie Myra passed on to me her 8mm ciné camera which she had decided she no longer wanted to keep. I had already become interested in photography, and even learned how to process films and produce enlargements, using the school dark-room. Now I branched out into amateur cinematography. Along with one or two friends I started a film club at the school. It was possible to hire both 8mm and 16mm films from John Martin's photographic shop in Hanley, which still had a Leek branch, so after-school film shows were arranged. We attempted to dub sound tracks to silent films, using a reel-to-reel tape-recorder, with music and other sound-effects generated on a record-player. Precise synchronisation of sound was never easy, but we produced some reasonable results. We also started to make a film record of various school activities and events over the space of a year. Though unfinished at the time I left LHS, it passed into the school archive, and more recently one of my former friends who was involved in the production, Alan Machin, kindly sent me a copy transferred to video.

In the summer of 1960 I was part of the group which went off on a visit to Austria and south Germany. A photograph taken of the group standing by the coach that was to take us to the ferry terminal shows us all smartly dressed in school uniform, which was *de rigueur* at least until we arrived on the other side of the Channel **[30]**. I made a ciné record of the whole trip, and we later added a sound-track to the edited version, using a record of Tyrolean music bought in Innsbruck for the purpose. I also wrote an article about the visit for the school magazine. Re-reading it now, I can see that by the age of seventeen I had developed a lucid and articulate style of descriptive writing. This was due in no small way to the excellent English teachers we had had, such as Tom Scott and T.R. Jones.

We were taught how to construct sentences, and how to analyse them into clauses, the correct use of the apostrophe and other basics of grammar which schools have since neglected, and with dire consequences in terms of falling standards of literacy.

It was at about this time that I joined the Leek and District Arts Club, which met in a specially-designated room in the Nicholson Institute in Stockwell Street. The Arts Club Room was furnished with spindle-back Windsor chairs, had its own small kitchen, and a kind of proscenium arch at the far end, under which was a grand piano. I joined mainly because of the photographic branch, but was drawn into the main body too. There were recitals, lectures by various visiting speakers on a wide range of arts-related subjects. John Betjeman visited twice to give poetry readings. As a lover of Victorian architecture, he was drawn to All Saints' Church, which he greatly admired. How odd it seems, on reflection, that a sixteen-year-old boy should have chosen to join a society composed of much older people devoted to serious subjects, instead of seeking the company of his peers. Leek seemed to have little to offer in the way of ready-made entertainment in those days. There were Saturday night dances (or 'hops') in St Mary's church hall, and I heard some of my contemporaries speak of 'going up to the Catholic', but I was never seriously tempted to join them, preferring instead to spend Saturday evenings with my books, history essays, and the radio for company. It was while I was in the sixth form that John Betjeman's verse autobiography, *Summoned by Bells,* was published. There was much in it with which I could identify: his shyness, his aversion to the sports-field and his love of architecture; the fact that he was bullied at school, and had an uneasy relationship with his father:

'An only child, deliciously apart,
Misunderstood and not like other boys...'

That most certainly resonated with me, as did the young

Betjeman's description of how he revelled in the delights of medieval churches:

> 'All that was crumbling, picturesque and quaint
> Informed my taste and sent me biking off,
> Escaped from games, for Architecture bound,
> Can words express the unexampled thrill
> I first enjoyed in Norm., E.E. and Dec.?
> Norm., crude and round and strong and primitive,
> E.E., so lofty, pointed, fine and pure,
> And Dec. the high perfection of it all,
> Flowingly curvilinear, from which
> The Perp. showed such a "lamentable decline".'

So I too visited, observed, noted, sketched and learned; so laying the foundations for what was to come in years ahead.

In the autumn of 1960 I had to make some decisions about what I might do after 'A' levels. The headmaster, Mr Pearce, thought I might have a budding vocation to the priesthood, and he suggested that I might test this by going to a weekend conference for prospective ordinands at Jesus College, Oxford. As I expected, this caused something of a rumpus at home. I can remember one rather unpleasant Sunday afternoon when Auntie Mary and Uncle John turned up, and they and my parents all had a 'go' at me. I remember Auntie Mary rubbing salt into the wounds by telling me in a very pointed way how lucky I was, what 'mummy and daddy' had sacrificed for me (yes, she really did talk down to me like that), and how I ought to show my eternal gratitude by doing what they wanted, and, conversely, by not doing what they didn't want. The memories of that afternoon, and the overwhelming sense of insecurity and resentment that it stirred up, are still etched upon my mind, and I think that today no self-respecting seventeen-year-old would tolerate such a confrontation without exploding. As it was, I possessed neither the will nor the wherewithal to retaliate: it was four against one, and in any case what was the point of arguing against minds that were already made up?

In the end I went to Oxford for the conference. It was after all externally financed and so did not involve my parents in any expenditure, and at least I got away on my own for a couple of days. Quite apart from the conference, and the opportunity of meeting like-minded people, Oxford was a most agreeable place in which to spend a little time, and there were opportunities to explore the city and the colleges. As to the main business of the conference, I came away with the feeling that – quite apart from the matter of parental opposition – this was something that I did not wish to pursue for the time being at any rate, and I have never regretted it. Experience of life in the outside world is, I believe, as essential a part of priestly formation as theological study in college.

What, then, was I going to do? As I have already said, careers advice was far from plentiful. Teaching was a possibility, but I would need to get into university or teacher-training college. What I really wanted to do, I suppose, was to pursue some kind of higher education which would involve history and/or languages, but I was not entirely sure what might come afterwards. In the autumn/winter of 1960 I sent off various application forms, in the first instance to various universities including Leicester and Hull. Various training colleges offered four-year external degree courses coupled with the teaching certificate, and I attended an interview at one of these – the College of St Mark & St John in Chelsea, but I failed to secure even a provisional place. My five 'O levels, and the lack of a science subject, did not give me the strongest of hands. Competition was tough, and it has to be remembered that in the early 1960s there were only about three dozen 'redbrick' universities in the U.K. Mr Conway, the history master, urged me to keep on trying, and his comment on one of my reports – 'He should not underestimate his academic ability' – gave me much encouragement. He had evidently spotted my potential in the essays I submitted to him, and in my general progress in the sixth. I did eventually secure a place at St Peter's College, Saltley, Birmingham, where one of my friends in the upper sixth, James Hollinshead, had already gone, but I have to say that I did not look forward to it with any great enthusiasm.

Mr Pearce's appointment as headmaster at LHS coincided more or less with the arrival of a new headmistress at Westwood Girls' High School, Miss Muriel Telford. Both had rather more enlightened ideas than their predecessors regarding the relationship between the two schools. Under the old régimes, there had been strict segregation; the premises of the one school were strictly out-of-bounds to members of the other. All this now began to change, at least at sixth form level. A joint Sixth Form Society was set up; there were joint meetings to which external speakers were invited; there were debates, and even (Wow!) social events such as end-of-term dances. I remember crossing for the first time the hallowed precincts of Westwood Hall for one such dance, held in the rather splendid setting of this neo-Elizabethan country house which, until it became a school, had been a private residence with a long and fascinating history. Some of us also went up into the town for ballroom-dancing classes held weekly in the Carr Gymnasium next the Nicholson Institute in Stockwell Street. They were presided over by Miss Margaret Galley (later Mrs Margaret Ryan). Thus a new world began to open up, although for me at any rate there were no special girl-friends at this time. With the possibility of a university place in prospect, it seemed hardly the right time to become involved in relationships – at least that is what I told myself. When I look back now on how I spent my spare time, I have no doubt that I missed out on certain things that my contemporaries enjoyed, and most certainly I was lacking in social skills. Saturday evenings, for example, were generally spent at home reading, writing and drawing, and listening to the radio, while others of my age would be out on the town, seeking whatever diversions were available in those days. Once past the age of eighteen, I did venture into one or two of the local pubs, and made a number of friends, but, at this stage, there were no girl-friends even though there were one or two who caught my eye.

Another of Mr Pearce's novelties was the introduction of a Champion House contest which was not confined to sporting events, so enabling those who were not particularly athletic to support their house in other ways. There was to be a creative writing competition, a music competition, and – unusually perhaps – a surveying competition. For the latter, each of the four houses had to raise a team to survey accurately the buildings and immediate precincts of Westwood Road Primary School, and then to draw up a scale plan. Equipment such as surveying chains, tapes, range-poles and even a plane table were made available through the geography department. This was something which had an obvious appeal to Geographical Society members. I gathered together a small surveying team for Hall House, and we submitted the winning entry. Likewise with the music competition, for which we were expected to put on a concert to include choral, vocal and instrumental items. I got a small choir together, and found a pianist, a clarinetist and a baritone soloist to perform individual items. The competition was judged by the headmaster's wife, a professional pianist who performed under her maiden name of Winifred Evans.

It was around this time that I became interested in golf. I suppose it began with games of pitch and putt on holidays, but here was a game that I thought I could really enjoy, and one that was not as highly competitive as some others. There was a small nine-hole course at Westwood to which a couple of friends of Auntie Nellie's belonged, and one of them offered to show me the basics, and take me round a few times. It was a challenging course, with hills, valleys, and a river hazard bordering three of the holes; but, with a few second-hand clubs to start with, and a junior membership fee of £1.10s (£1.50) a year, I quickly took to it. One or two others from school joined as well – James Hollinshead, Andrew Bould, and some of the staff, such as D.N.Jones whose woodworking talents later made him a particularly useful member of the club. A lot of my spare time was spent on the golf course, and for a time it also seriously affected my church attendance. One Sunday morning, as I was heading for the golf course on my bike, I encountered my godmother, Auntie Flossie, who was walking in the opposite direction towards St Edward's Church. We stopped and talked for a few moments. She knew where I was going of course, and I remember her drawing my attention to the sound of the distant church bells in full peal. 'That's where I'm going,' she said. 'Perhaps one day they'll call you back too.' And so they did; not the following week nor the week after, but not so very long afterwards. I have never forgotten my godmother's kindly words which brought me back into the fold, as it were, and I know that if I had not heeded them my life might have followed a very different course.

Meanwhile, the A-level exams drew ever closer, and I was determined to do as well as I could. Evenings and weekends became increasing crammed with revision and extra reading. 'A' level examinations involved sitting two or more written papers for each subject. The history papers were in British and European history, and answers were written out in essay form. Modern languages involved the study of set texts. The Latin ones included Virgil and Cicero, while for French we studies Alain-Fournier's *Le Grand Meaulnes*, Molière's *L'Avare,* and Balzac's *Eugénie Grandet.* The French examinations involved both aural and oral tests, so spoken French was important. There was a French *assistant* who ran the conversation group. He was Guy DeSanti who came from the south of France, and who found the North Staffordshire winter more than a trifle challenging, especially as he had to sleep in an unheated bedroom – something unheard of in France, so he told us. He was a keen supporter of President Charles de Gaulle, and was vehemently opposed to Algerian independence. I kept in touch with him by letter after he left LHS at the end of the year, and after the letters suddenly stopped I discovered that he had been killed while on military service. Then there was Mademoiselle, the glamorous young *assistante* who followed, and who created rather a stir. Many who had opted not to continue with French now wished that they had!

After taking all the exams, the summer term – and indeed my six years at LHS – came to an end with a whimper rather than a bang, since we officially left once 'A' level study-leave began, and thereafter came into school only on examinations days. All was provisional, however, until after the results came out in the middle of August. On that particular morning Dad was at home ill and in bed when I walked up to school to find out how I had fared, and to join the queue outside the headmaster's study. We were called in individually, and Mr Pearce communicated the results verbally, adding his own comments. To my surprise and delight I learned that I had passed all three of my main subjects, plus the general studies paper which everyone was obliged to take as a counterbalance to the over-specialisation of most sixth-form courses. An A-level pass in general studies was deemed by many universities to compensate for any single deficiency at O-level – e.g. maths, or another science, or a foreign language. Although I had re-taken maths in the lower sixth, I never passed at O-level, but the general studies A-level meant that I now had all the basic university entrance requirements. 'Perhaps your Uncle John will be satisfied now,' D.N. Jones said to me later, knowing what my uncle's attitude could sometimes be like.

Uncle John was not the only one to have been surprised. It silenced a lot of other 'doubting Thomases' too. When I got home and told my parents, Dad immediately decided to go and see Mr Pearce himself. To my knowledge that was the only occasion on which my father had gone up to the school to see a member of staff. Although mother was involved with the Parents' Association, and a member of the committee while I was in the sixth form, Dad didn't believe in such things, and he had kept his distance. Now this suddenly changed, and that was not all. From now on my relationship with Dad changed as well. He began to see me as a young adult, and as one who had, in spite of certain disadvantages, done rather well for himself, and though he was a man of few words when it came to expressing feelings, the smile said it all, and I think he was rather proud. I don't know precisely what he said to Mr Pearce, except that when the headmaster pointed out that I had a place at Saltley College, he came out with something like, 'Saltley be b******d!'

Following further conversations with Mr Pearce and Mr Conway, it was agreed that I would return to school in September, take some S-level papers, re-apply to universities and also have a shot at Oxford or Cambridge. There was even the possibility that a university place might suddenly become available that very autumn because of the movements and re-allocations that inevitably took place after A-level results were published. So I re-applied to Leicester which had been my first choice anyway, and I was called for interview by Professor Simmons of the history department.

Just before the start of the new term, Auntie Mary and Uncle John celebrated their silver wedding anniversary. They had been married on September 3rd 1936, and this was also the anniversary of the outbreak of World War II in 1939 – a fact that sometimes produced wry comments. Auntie Mary took the anniversary (wedding, that is) very seriously every year, expecting members of the family to visit, and Uncle John would always arrange for a bunch of red carnations, one for each year of their marriage, to be delivered to the house. The silver wedding was therefore likely to be celebrated in grand style, and so it was, with a big gathering of relatives and friends at the Southbank Hotel. Amongst the guests were Uncle John's elderly parents who still lived in Mansfield, and the oldest living member of the Carding family, great-aunt Sarah, my grandmother's youngest sister. It was a formal occasion too, and I think this was the first time I wore a dinner-jacket, as most of the men did **[31]**.

A few days later I returned to Leek High School. I also started to attend Mr Conway's evening classes in economics at the College of Further Education. He thought that this extra subject would be useful. Mr Lazarus acquired the necessary texts for S-level French, so we made a start on those. It was in fact during one of Mr Lazarus' tutorial sessions with me in the library one morning – and I can clearly remember that we were reading Molière's *Le Médecin Malgré Lui* – that a message came that I was to go to the headmaster's study. My mother was there, with a telegram that had been delivered that morning. It was from Professor Simmons offering me a place at Leicester to read History. It was almost the end of September, and if I took up the offer I would have just about a week in which to get ready.

I needed to weigh things up carefully, and to talk over with the head and with others the advantages and disadvantages of taking what was on offer now and therefore forfeiting the opportunity of trying for Oxbridge. I had liked what I had seen of Leicester at the time of my interview, and so I decided to take up the offer. 'What am I going to do with those texts now?' said Mr Lazarus with a wry smile when I told him that I was leaving. Goodbyes were said rather hurriedly, and I had to turn my attention very rapidly to preparing to go away from home for the first time. The family were of course delighted, the only fly in the ointment being Auntie Mary who said that I wouldn't have got there if somebody else hadn't dropped out, making me half wish that I had decided to stay on at school and have a shot at Oxbridge. What did I have to do in order to prove myself to some people? This is a question that has returned to haunt me from time to time when

I have found myself up against those who – for whatever reason – have tried to undermine my confidence or who have doubted my capabilities.

Looking back over my life, I realise how very much I owe to those formative years at Leek High School. I missed some opportunities of course. I regret not having persevered more at maths, I wish I had taken more interest in team games such as rugby, and I think I could have done better at 'O' level with a bit more determination, and a less stressful adolescence; but it would seem that I was something of a late-developer, and it was in the sixth form that I really came into my own. The key influences were of course Mr Lazarus and Mr Metcalfe for French, Mr Glenny the classics master, and of course Mr Conway, but the influence of several teachers whose subjects I did not pursue also remained for a very long time. There was Victor Middlemas, whose enthusiasm could make a dry subject like physics seem interesting, and he was much involved with the drama productions that I took part in. There were the art teachers from whom I learned basic drawing techniques that have been called upon at various times in my life; while the surveying methods learned at LHS have proved useful in measuring up historic buildings and drawing scale plans and elevations. It was at school that I learned what would now be called 'desk-top publishing' and keyboard skills, how to edit and produce a small magazine, how to process a film and make enlargements, music appreciation too – all of these extra-curricular pursuits broadened my education. Lower down in the school I was regarded as something of a loner, and I think there have always been times when I have needed to be left alone; but I was also able to get along happily with most people, to work as part of a group, and several of the friendships established during those years at LHS have stood the test of time. Partly because of my own experiences at Leek High School, I have always supported the grammar school system against the detractors who were hell-bent (I use the term advisedly) on its total abolition on the grounds of 'elitism'. Such schools offered – and still do where they survive – to any boy or girl who is academically inclined, regardless of social background or parental resources, the opportunity of an education suited to their educational development, and it is primarily to do with education, and not social engineering. As I remember it, the social mix at Leek High School embraced town and country boys, sons of skilled and unskilled workers, professionals, shopkeepers and shop-workers, and 'class' never seemed to enter into it.

Dear Octopus is the title of a comedy-drama written in the late 1930s by Dodie Smith, and a favourite with amateur dramatic societies of which there were two or three in Leek and the surrounding area. The play concerns the interaction between four generations of a particular family, and the title comes from a line in the play referring to the family as a 'dear octopus from whose tentacles we never quite escape'. Family, by which I mean primarily my mother's family, was certainly a dominant influence in my childhood and teenage years; we were very close. Therefore I became imbued with their ideas and standards and outlooks which – given that they had all been born in late-Victorian or Edwardian England – were necessarily those of an earlier age, 'old-fashioned' some would say. Consequently I found myself, wittingly or unwittingly, clutching at the coat-tails of an England that was soon to disappear. The early sixties were when things began to change. Casual dress for men still meant shirt and tie, sports jacket and flannels; jeans were what bricklayers and plumbers wore to work. My father was a 'blue-collar' worker, but would never dream of going out of an evening without a jacket and tie, and the weekday cloth cap gave way to a smart trilby. Ladies still routinely wore hats and gloves **[32]**. Signs of change there were, however, amongst the younger generation; the 'Teddy Boy' phenomenon of the 1950s, the influence of American 'pop' culture beginning to take effect in the U.K., and the emergence of a distinctive and rebellious teenage culture. For the time being, however, most things remained the same: university students were on the whole well-behaved, well-dressed, and as yet largely unpoliticised, and although CND was beginning to gain ground, student protest movements were still a thing of the future, as was long hair for males.

Looking back on those far-off days in Leek, I am rather glad to have been blessed with a childhood that was 'out of the noise' in more senses than one. Childhood was just that: there were few if any of the problems, pressures and challenges that children of the early twenty-first century appear to labour under, such as knife-crime, gambling addiction, drink- and drug-related issues, with ever-growing recourse to social workers and psychiatrists. Compared with these, my unhappy experiences during adolescence, though regrettable, seem slight and transitory, and there were many compensating factors.

My time as a university student and the life-long friendships I made during those years away from Leek, is another story, but I have summarised it in the Postscript. Suffice it to say here that, throughout my undergraduate years, I came home only once during term time. That was in late November 1961 when I returned to Leek High School to collect my A-level certificates at the annual Speech Day. In fact I crossed the stage four times: once to collect the certificates, and thrice more to receive the prizes for history, French and Latin. In the words of Benjamin Disraeli, I had indeed 'climbed to the top of the greasy pole', and so cocked a snook at those who had previously underestimated me or tried to intimidate me. On her copy of the programme, my mother wrote 'Grand Slam Day', and for the first time ever, my father took time off work to attend an event at the school. At last, it seemed, I had won his approval and his accolade. That meant more to me than all the prizes and certificates in the world.

POSTSCRIPT

How quickly I settled in at Leicester University was something of a surprise to me as well as to many who knew me, as I had never been away from home before for any length of time. It was all very new and exciting. There was the pre-sessional congress organised by the Students' Union, at which a multiplicity of clubs and societies set up their stall to attract new members. Then there was the Hall of Residence – in my case Digby Hall. The university had had the foresight to acquire several large houses in the 'stockbrokers' belt' at Oadby, a couple of miles south-west of the city centre, each one of which had spacious grounds on which purpose-built student accommodation blocks and refectories could be sited. Digby House was one of these, built in 1907 in Tudor-Gothic style. Being so far removed from the university campus, the halls had a social life of their own, with a Junior Common Room Committee. I quickly became involved with this, and in my third year was elected JCR secretary. I also joined the university dramatic society, and took part in debates. Earlier experiences during my time at Leek High School no doubt stood me in good stead. I made many new friends, some of whom were to become friends for life.

The warden of Digby Hall was James Crompton, an Oxford history graduate and a B.Litt., who had held a lectureship at Grahamstown University, S.A., before returning to England in the summer of 1961 to take up this new appointment. Though only in his mid-forties, he looked much older, with receding white hair. Not only was he an historian (and a medievalist at that); he had an encyclopaedic knowledge of architecture, loved classical music, and was an active church member of the Anglo-Catholic kind. Thus he became something of a father figure and a role model with whom I could share my enthusiasm for those very subjects which my own father had dismissed as useless. It was James Crompton who took me, along with some other students, on my first-ever visit to the Shrine of Our Lady of Walsingham in Norfolk, for the 1963 National Pilgrimage.

Pleasant as were these activities and diversions, I was at Leicester first and foremost to work for my degree. Lectures and tutorials occupied some of the time, with long spells of private study in the library and back in hall, and essay-writing. In the course of a lecture on the deposition of King Richard II, the lecturer referred to the Chronicle of Dieulacres Abbey. Instead of the familiar 'Dieu-la-cress', he pronounced it 'Dew-laykers' which puzzled me at first, until it dawned on me that he meant the abbey at Leek which had aroused my childhood interest. This interest now deepened as I learned how significant was this fourteenth-century document (kept in the library of Gray's Inn, London) in revealing what actually happened to this ill-fated king. I began to delve more deeply into the abbey's history, using the local history facilities of the university library.

In the summer of 1962 I bought my first car: a 1948 Austin 8 which cost me £60 out of my life's savings. It gave me the freedom to explore, along with some like-minded friends, the delightful villages of Leicestershire and Rutland, and so extend my architectural knowledge. We ventured even further afield. On a Sunday morning, at some unearthly hour, we set off for London via the M1 to attend High Mass at All Saints', Margaret Street, the model church of the Victorian ecclesiologists. Having chosen the mid-Victorian age as my special paper, I came to learn more of the architect of those north Staffordshire buildings I had known and loved since childhood: A.W.N. Pugin.

I sat my finals in the summer of 1964, and gained a II(i) honours degree. I returned to Leicester in the autumn to do a PGCE in the education department. I must confess that teaching was something that I drifted towards with no great enthusiasm. In those days there wasn't much careers advice to draw upon. My true inclination was towards historical research and writing, and the 'Ed. Year' enabled me to pursue these interests in my spare time. Then in the Spring of 1965 I was informed that a number of research studentships in history were available on application at Keele University. I had a research topic already mapped out, i.e. Dieulacres Abbey, which of course was local to Keele, so I applied, was called for interview and was awarded a two-year studentship leading to a master's degree.

In July 1965 I said farewell to Leicester University in a – literally – dramatic way. The Drama Society had booked the Falmouth Arts Theatre for two weeks to stage a production of Jean Anouilh's *The Waltz of the Toreadors,* in which I was to play one of the principal roles. So off to Cornwall we all went, and in between rehearsals and performances there was time for beach parties, sightseeing and other activities in glorious summer weather.

Leaving Leicester was a huge emotional wrench. My four years there had been blissfully happy, blighted only by the lingering memory of lost love, but that's another story. In addition to gaining an honours degree I had grown in self-confidence and also made some new and lasting friendships. Keele was altogether a different experience. Being a research student meant spending a lot of time on my own, with only an occasional meeting with my supervisor, and there didn't seem to be the kind of social life that

I had enjoyed so much at Digby Hall. It also meant travelling out to archive repositories in London, Oxford and Chester, and doing some field work on various sites. My thesis was complete and ready for presentation in May 1967, but on the day I presented it I received the devastating news that my supervisor, Hugh Leech, had died suddenly that very morning. This took the shine off the degree ceremony a month later when I received my M.A. from H.R.H. Princess Margaret as Chancellor of Keele.

Dieulacres Abbey is a subject that refuses to go away. An abridged version of my thesis was published in 1969, a more extended version somewhat later, and a revised edition as recently as 2015. Invitations to give talks on the subject to local history groups still come in from time to time; also enquiries about aspects of the abbey's history from people undertaking their own research.

A double-degree man without a job: that's where I stood in June 1967. James Crompton drew my attention to a research post with the Victoria County History in Wiltshire, but I didn't fancy moving so far away from home ground; so far had I slipped back into the arms of that 'dear octopus' that was my – now ageing – family. Instead I took up an appointment as assistant history master at King Edward VI Grammar School in Stafford. It would, I thought, tide me over until I could decide where exactly my professional career was heading. It proved to be a good choice. Within two years I was promoted to second in the department, and a year later became head of History. Meanwhile, I had met and married Isobel, who came from Blythe Bridge, and we set up home in Stafford where our daughter Sarah was born and raised. Stafford has been our home ever since. My promotion to head of department was offset by the death of my father in May 1970, a few weeks before what would have been his sixtieth birthday, having been diagnosed with terminal cancer. One consolation was that he had lived long enough to see his grand-daughter Sarah past her first birthday, and he loved her.

Uncle John Asher died in November of the same year; then, one by one, the rest of that generation: Auntie Dorothy in 1971, and Auntie Nellie died suddenly in the summer of 1975 while visiting St Edward's Church. Aunts Flossie and Myra died in 1983, Mary Asher in 1986, and finally my mother – who described herself as 'the last pebble on the beach' – in 1990.

It was in the 1970s that earlier thoughts about ordination to the priesthood re-surfaced, following one or two promptings from a local clergyman who thought I had a vocation and challenged me to test it. In 1975 I attended a bishops' selection conference, and was recommended for training for the non-stipendiary priesthood, a scheme similar to the 'worker-priest' system operating within the Catholic Church in France. Theological training is undertaken on a part-time basis and the ordinand remains in secular employment, serving – post-ordination – as an assistant priest in his home parish. Following a three-year course at The Queen's College, Birmingham, I was ordained deacon in July 1978, and priest a year later, in Lichfield Cathedral. Thus another seed planted during those boyhood days in Leek came finally to fruition. For nigh on 35 years I served as a non-stipendiary assistant priest in the Parish of Stafford, and latterly as priest-in-charge of the 12th-century church of St Chad, Stafford's principal Anglo-Catholic church, in the centre of the town.

Disillusionment with the seemingly endless changes in the educational system in Stafford following the abolition of both the boys' and girls' grammar schools in the late 1970s led me eventually to quit teaching and to join the ranks of the self-employed. In 1998 I set up a small craft workshop producing ornamental carving and lettering in Welsh slate; a skill I had taught myself over several years, and which had become something more than just a hobby. Commissions for chisel-cut inscriptions and, eventually, memorial headstones, came my way, some of them through the Diocesan Advisory Committee who were aware that one of the priests of the diocese was also a memorial artist. One such was a bilingual French/English inscription on a new memorial to Napoleonic prisoners of war who had lived in cottages close to St Edward's Church, Leek, and who lay buried in the churchyard not far from some of the older Carding family graves. This commission seemed to bring together my historical and linguistic interests, craftmanship, and family connections with St Edward's. I have always had strong feeling that the slate-carving skills came to me partly through my grandfather, Clifford Keates, and my father, both of whom were immensely talented craftsmen in wood and metal.

At the same time I resumed historical research and writing, principally in the realm of Victorian architecture and the Gothic Revival, homing in on the life and work of the Victorian architect A.W.N. Pugin. Several publications helped to boost my income, along with invitations to lecture to various groups and societies, and to organise 'Pugin-land' tours to Alton, Cheadle, and other related sites in Staffordshire. There was an obvious overlap between my excursions into church history and my priestly ministry as I was able to appreciate and express the theological foundations of Pugin's work. 'Literary ministry' was how one clergyman kindly described it, and of course it was supporting my unpaid parochial ministry as well as putting food on the table.

The artistic legacy of Pugin was being kept alive by the Birmingham firm of John Hardman & Co. Founded in 1838 by John Hardman Jnr. at Pugin's instigation, the firm was still producing stained glass in the Gothic style, and held a sizeable archive collection in addition to those deposited in the Birmingham Library and Museum. I was invited to begin classifying this material, and so became their consultant archivist, also handling enquiries which came in from churches and from individuals seeking information about historic Hardman glass. I was also commissioned to undertake an attics-to-cellars survey of the historic buildings at Alton Towers, research their history and produce a report which would inform and guide future restoration projects. This formed the basis of my published work on Alton Towers which ran to several editions and reprints. Several other publications followed, the latest – *Guarding the Pugin Flame* (Spire Books, 2017) – taking the Pugin story to the next generation through the life and work of his only pupil (and son-in-law), John Hardman Powell. Election to a Fellowship of the Society of Antiquaries of London in 2006 marked the summit of my academic career.

Self-employment enabled me to adopt a more flexible approach to my parochial ministry. Weekday Masses and daytime visiting were now possible in a way they had not been while I was still teaching. In 2013, having reached the age of 70, I retired from St Chad's. Retirement from the parish does not, however, mean release from one's priestly vows. The parish priest of SS Michael & All Angels', Cross Heath, Newcastle-under-Lyme, who had become a personal friend, invited me to join him at the altar both there and at his other church, St Paul's, Newcastle. That has proved to be a great blessing to both Isobel and me; in fact a new lease of the priestly life. On my first visit to St Paul's I was surprised to see a photograph of a former vicar of St Edward's, Prebendary Norman Watson, who, I now discovered, had been vicar of St Paul's in the 1920s. There was also a brass plaque commemorating his five years' incumbency there. So another bit of my past had caught up with me, as it was Prebendary Watson who had first awakened my interest in Dieulacres Abbey and the history of St Edward's Church. If today I am able to pitch a note accurately, point the Psalms correctly, or sing the musical parts of the Mass competently, it is on account of the basic musical training I received all those years ago as a member of St Edward's choir. Later on, at All Saints' Church, I was trained as an altar-server by Fr. Norman Turner (parish priest 1952-1966), who not only showed me how things should be done at the altar, but why, and what it all means. By observation, I learned as much from Fr. Turner about the proper conduct of worship as I did later in theological college, and it has remained with me throughout my own priestly ministry.

My interest in the Welsh language also goes back to those boyhood years in Leek. Our daughter now lives in South Wales, having moved there in 1996 on account of her husband's new job, and we now have two Welsh-born and Welsh-speaking grandsons, so there's every incentive for me to *siarad yr Iaith.* So, as I look back over the fifty years since I left my home town, I see how almost every aspect of my life and varied career has been shaped by those formative years in Leek 'out of the noise', and I shall remain for ever grateful to those who made it all possible.